RStudio for R Statistical Computing Cookbook

Over 50 practical and useful recipes to help you perform data analysis with R by unleashing every native RStudio feature

Andrea Cirillo

BIRMINGHAM - MUMBAI

RStudio for R Statistical Computing Cookbook

First published: April 2016

Production reference: 1250416

Published by Packt Publishing Ltd.
Livery Place
35 Livery Street
Birmingham B3 2PB, UK.

ISBN 978-1-78439-103-4

www.packtpub.com

Credits

Author
Andrea Cirillo

Reviewer
Mark van der Loo

Commissioning Editor
Kartikey Pandey

Acquisition Editor
Vinay Argekar

Content Development Editor
Deepti Thore

Technical Editor
Madhunikita Sunil Chindarkar

Copy Editor
Karuna Narayan

Project Coordinator
Shweta H Birwatkar

Proofreader
Safis Editing

Indexer
Rekha Nair

Graphics
Disha Haria

Production Coordinator
Aparna Bhagat

Cover Work
Aparna Bhagat

About the Author

Andrea Cirillo is currently working as an internal auditor at Intesa Sanpaolo banking group. He gained a lot of financial and external audit experience at Deloitte Touche Tohmatsu and internal audit experience at FNM, a listed Italian company.

His current main responsibilities involve evaluation of credit risk management models and their enhancement mainly within the field of the Basel III capital agreement.

He is married to Francesca and is the father of Tommaso, Gianna, and Zaccaria.

Andrea has written and contributed to a few useful R packages and regularly shares insightful advice and tutorials about R programming.

His research and work mainly focuses on the use of R in the fields of risk management and fraud detection, mainly through modeling custom algorithms and developing interactive applications.

This book is the result of a lot of patience by my wife and sons, which left me with the time to write this book, the time that I should have spend with them.

By Deepti Thore, my content developer editor at Packt Publishing, who was so clement with me when, and it happened a lot of time, I missed my writing deadlines.

By my colleagues who endured my talks about the book every three hours and when I asked for their opinions about almost every recipe.

To all of you, I would like to say a sincere thank you.

About the Reviewer

Mark van der Loo is a statistical researcher who specializes in data cleaning methodology and likes to program in R and C. He is the author and coauthor of several R packages published on CRAN, including stringdist, validate, deductive, lintools, and several others. In 2012, he authored *Learning RStudio for R Statistical Computing, Packt Publishing,* with Edwin de Jonge.

www.PacktPub.com

eBooks, discount offers, and more

Did you know that Packt offers eBook versions of every book published, with PDF and ePub files available? You can upgrade to the eBook version at www.PacktPub.com and as a print book customer, you are entitled to a discount on the eBook copy. Get in touch with us at customercare@packtpub.com for more details.

At www.PacktPub.com, you can also read a collection of free technical articles, sign up for a range of free newsletters and receive exclusive discounts and offers on Packt books and eBooks.

https://www2.packtpub.com/books/subscription/packtlib

Do you need instant solutions to your IT questions? PacktLib is Packt's online digital book library. Here, you can search, access, and read Packt's entire library of books.

Why Subscribe?

- ▶ Fully searchable across every book published by Packt
- ▶ Copy and paste, print, and bookmark content
- ▶ On demand and accessible via a web browser

Table of Contents

Preface   **v**

Chapter 1: Acquiring Data for Your Project   **1**

Introduction   1

Acquiring data from the Web – web scraping tasks   2

Accessing an API with R   12

Getting data from Twitter with the twitteR package   16

Getting data from Facebook with the Rfacebook package   21

Getting data from Google Analytics   24

Loading your data into R with rio packages   27

Converting file formats using the rio package   31

Chapter 2: Preparing for Analysis – Data Cleansing and Manipulation   **33**

Introduction   33

Getting a sense of your data structure with R   34

Preparing your data for analysis with the tidyr package   36

Detecting and removing missing values   40

Substituting missing values using the mice package   43

Detecting and removing outliers   47

Performing data filtering activities   48

Chapter 3: Basic Visualization Techniques   **59**

Introduction   59

Looking at your data using the plot() function   60

Using pairs.panel() to look at (visualize) correlations between variables   67

Adding text to a ggplot2 plot at a custom location   69

Changing axes appearance to ggplot2 plot (continous axes)   74

Producing a matrix of graphs with ggplot2   79

Drawing a route on a map with ggmap   85

Making use of the igraph package to draw a network   88

Showing communities in a network with the linkcomm package   93

Chapter 4: Advanced and Interactive Visualization — 99

Introduction — 99
Producing a Sankey diagram with the networkD3 package — 100
Creating a dynamic force network with the visNetwork package — 104
Building a rotating 3D graph and exporting it as a GIF — 110
Using the DiagrammeR package to produce a process flow diagram in RStudio — 112

Chapter 5: Power Programming with R — 117

Introduction — 117
Writing modular code in RStudio — 118
Implementing parallel computation in R — 120
Creating custom objects and methods in R using the S3 system — 123
Evaluating your code performance using the profvis package — 126
Comparing an alternative function's performance using the microbenchmarking package — 129
Using GitHub with RStudio — 131

Chapter 6: Domain-specific Applications — 141

Introduction — 142
Dealing with regular expressions — 142
Analyzing PDF reports in a folder with the tm package — 143
Creating word clouds with the wordcloud package — 148
Performing a Twitter sentiment analysis — 151
Detecting fraud in e-commerce orders with Benford's law — 156
Measuring customer retention using cohort analysis in R — 161
Making a recommendation engine — 163
Performing time series decomposition using the stl() function — 165
Exploring time series forecasting with forecast() — 167
Tracking stock movements using the quantmod package — 168
Optimizing portfolio composition and maximising returns with the Portfolio Analytics package — 170
Forecasting the stock market — 173

Chapter 7: Developing Static Reports — 175

Introduction — 175
Using one markup language for all types of documents – rmarkdown — 177
Writing and styling PDF documents with RStudio — 184
Writing wonderful tufte handouts with the tufte package and rmarkdown — 186
Sharing your code and plots with slides — 188
Curating a blog through RStudio — 190

Chapter 8: Dynamic Reporting and Web Application Development   197

Introduction   197
Generating dynamic parametrized reports with R Markdown   198
Developing a single-file Shiny app   204
Changing a Shiny app UI based on user input   209
Creating an interactive report with Shiny   213
Constructing RStudio add-ins   216
Sharing your work on RPubs   220
Deploying your app on Amazon AWS with ramazon   222

Index   225

Preface

Why should you read *RStudio for R Statistical Computing Cookbook?*

Well, even if there are plenty of books and blog posts about R and RStudio out there, this cookbook can be an unbeatable friend through your journey from being an average R and RStudio user to becoming an advanced and effective R programmer.

I have collected more than 50 recipes here, covering the full spectrum of data analysis activities, from data acquisition and treatment to results reporting.

All of them come from my direct experience as an auditor and data analyst and from knowledge sharing with the really dynamic and always growing R community.

I took great care selecting and highlighting those packages and practices that have proven to be the best for a given particular task, sometimes choosing between different packages designed for the same purpose.

You can therefore be sure that what you will learn here is the cutting edge of the R language and will place you on the right track of your learning path to R's mastery.

What this book covers

Chapter 1, Acquiring Data for Your Project, shows you how to import data into the R environment, taking you through web scraping and the process of connecting to an API.

Chapter 2, Preparing for Analysis – Data Cleansing and Manipulation, teaches you how to get your data ready for analysis, leveraging the latest data-handling packages and advanced statistical techniques for missing values and outlier treatments.

Chapter 3, Basic Visualization Techniques, lets you get the first sense of your data, highlighting its structure and discovering patterns within it.

Chapter 4, Advanced and Interactive Visualization, shows you how to produce advanced visualizations ranging from 3D graphs to animated plots.

Chapter 5, Power Programming with R, discusses how to write efficient R code, making use of the R objective-oriented systems and advanced tools for code performance evaluation.

Chapter 6, Domain-specific Applications, shows you how to apply the R language to a wide range of problems related to different domains, from financial portfolio optimization to e-commerce fraud detection.

Chapter 7, Developing Static Reports, helps you discover the reporting tools available within the RStudio IDE and how to make the most of them to produce static reports for sharing results of your work.

Chapter 8, Dynamic Reporting and Web Application Development, displays the collected recipes designed to make use of the latest features introduced in RStudio from shiny web applications with dynamic UIs to RStudio add-ons.

What you need for this book

The basic requirements for this book are the latest versions of R and RStudio, which you can download from the following URLs:

- ▶ For Windows: `https://cran.r-project.org/bin/windows/base/`
- ▶ For Mac OS X: `https://cran.r-project.org/bin/macosx/`
- ▶ `https://www.rstudio.com/products/rstudio/download/`

More software will be needed for a few specific recipes, which will be highlighted in the *Getting Ready* section of the respective recipe.

Just a closing note: all the software employed in this book is available for free for personal use, and the greatest advantage of them is that they are open source and powered by the R community.

Who this book is for

This book was developed and written keeping in mind an average R and RStudio user who would like to make the move from good to great in the field of their programming skills on the language.

If you think you are quite good at R and RStudio but you are still missing something in order to be great, this book is exactly what you need to read.

Sections

In this book, you will find several headings that appear frequently (Getting ready, How to do it, How it works, There's more, and See also).

To give clear instructions on how to complete a recipe, we use these sections as follows:

Getting ready

This section tells you what to expect in the recipe, and describes how to set up any software or any preliminary settings required for the recipe.

How to do it...

This section contains the steps required to follow the recipe.

How it works...

This section usually consists of a detailed explanation of what happened in the previous section.

There's more...

This section consists of additional information about the recipe in order to make the reader more knowledgeable about the recipe.

See also

This section provides helpful links to other useful information for the recipe.

Conventions

In this book, you will find a number of text styles that distinguish between different kinds of information. Here are some examples of these styles and an explanation of their meaning.

Code words in text, database table names, folder names, filenames, file extensions, pathnames, dummy URLs, user input, and Twitter handles are shown as follows: "The `plot()` function is one of most powerful functions in base R."

A block of code is set as follows:

```
> str(lesmiserables)
'data.frame':  254 obs. of  2 variables:
 $ V1: Factor w/ 73 levels "Anzelma","Babet",..: 61 49 55 55 21 33 12
23 20 62 ...
 $ V2: Factor w/ 49 levels "Babet","Bahorel",..: 42 42 42 36 42 42 42
42 42 42 ...
```

Any command-line input or output is written as follows:

```
install.packages("linkcomm")

library(linkcomm)
```

New terms and **important words** are shown in bold. Words that you see on the screen, for example, in menus or dialog boxes, appear in the text like this: "In order to embed your Sankey diagram, you can leverage the RStudio **Save as Web Page** control from the **Export** menu."

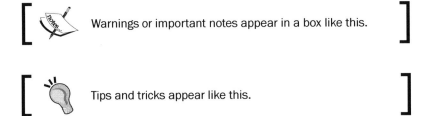

Warnings or important notes appear in a box like this.

Tips and tricks appear like this.

Reader feedback

Feedback from our readers is always welcome. Let us know what you think about this book—what you liked or disliked. Reader feedback is important for us as it helps us develop titles that you will really get the most out of.

To send us general feedback, simply e-mail feedback@packtpub.com, and mention the book's title in the subject of your message.

If there is a topic that you have expertise in and you are interested in either writing or contributing to a book, see our author guide at www.packtpub.com/authors.

Customer support

Now that you are the proud owner of a Packt book, we have a number of things to help you to get the most from your purchase.

Downloading the example code

You can download the example code files for this book from your account at `http://www.packtpub.com`. If you purchased this book elsewhere, you can visit `http://www.packtpub.com/support` and register to have the files e-mailed directly to you.

You can download the code files by following these steps:

1. Log in or register to our website using your e-mail address and password.
2. Hover the mouse pointer on the **SUPPORT** tab at the top.
3. Click on **Code Downloads & Errata**.
4. Enter the name of the book in the **Search** box.
5. Select the book for which you're looking to download the code files.
6. Choose from the drop-down menu where you purchased this book from.
7. Click on **Code Download**.

You can also download the code files by clicking on the **Code Files** button on the book's webpage at the Packt Publishing website. This page can be accessed by entering the book's name in the **Search** box. Please note that you need to be logged in to your Packt account.

Once the file is downloaded, please make sure that you unzip or extract the folder using the latest version of:

▸ WinRAR / 7-Zip for Windows
▸ Zipeg / iZip / UnRarX for Mac
▸ 7-Zip / PeaZip for Linux

Downloading the color images of this book

We also provide you with a PDF file that has color images of the screenshots/diagrams used in this book. The color images will help you better understand the changes in the output. You can download this file from `https://www.packtpub.com/sites/default/files/downloads/RStudioforRStatisticalComputingCookbook_ColorImages.pdf`.

Errata

Although we have taken every care to ensure the accuracy of our content, mistakes do happen. If you find a mistake in one of our books—maybe a mistake in the text or the code—we would be grateful if you could report this to us. By doing so, you can save other readers from frustration and help us improve subsequent versions of this book. If you find any errata, please report them by visiting http://www.packtpub.com/submit-errata, selecting your book, clicking on the **Errata Submission Form** link, and entering the details of your errata. Once your errata are verified, your submission will be accepted and the errata will be uploaded to our website or added to any list of existing errata under the Errata section of that title.

To view the previously submitted errata, go to https://www.packtpub.com/books/content/support and enter the name of the book in the search field. The required information will appear under the **Errata** section.

Piracy

Piracy of copyrighted material on the Internet is an ongoing problem across all media. At Packt, we take the protection of our copyright and licenses very seriously. If you come across any illegal copies of our works in any form on the Internet, please provide us with the location address or website name immediately so that we can pursue a remedy.

Please contact us at copyright@packtpub.com with a link to the suspected pirated material.

We appreciate your help in protecting our authors and our ability to bring you valuable content.

Questions

If you have a problem with any aspect of this book, you can contact us at questions@packtpub.com, and we will do our best to address the problem.

1
Acquiring Data for Your Project

In this chapter, we will cover the following recipes:

- ▶ Acquiring data from the Web—web scraping tasks
- ▶ Accessing an API with R
- ▶ Getting data from Twitter with the `twitteR` package
- ▶ Getting data from Facebook with the `Rfacebook` package
- ▶ Getting data from Google Analytics
- ▶ Loading your data into R with `rio` packages
- ▶ Converting file formats using the `rio` package

Introduction

The American statistician Edward Deming once said:

"Without data you are just another man with an opinion."

I think this great quote is enough to highlight the importance of the data acquisition phase of every data analysis project. This phase is exactly where we are going to start from. This chapter will give you tools for scraping the Web, accessing data via web APIs, and importing nearly every kind of file you will probably have to work with quickly, thanks to the magic package `rio`.

All the recipes in this book are based on the great and popular packages developed and maintained by the members of the R community.

After reading this section, you will be able to get all your data into R to start your data analysis project, no matter where it comes from.

Before starting the data acquisition process, you should gain a clear understanding of your data needs. In other words, what data do you need in order to get solutions to your problems?

A rule of thumb to solve this problem is to look at the process that you are investigating—from input to output—and outline all the data that will go in and out during its development.

In this data, you will surely have that chunk of data that is needed to solve your problem.

In particular, for each type of data you are going to acquire, you should define the following:

> ▸ **The source**: This is where data is stored
>
> ▸ **The required authorizations**: This refers to any form of authorization/authentication that is needed in order to get the data you need
>
> ▸ **The data format**: This is the format in which data is made available
>
> ▸ **The data license**: This is to check whether there is any license covering data utilization/distribution or whether there is any need for ethics/privacy considerations

After covering these points for each set of data, you will have a clear vision of future data acquisition activities. This will let you plan ahead the activities needed to clearly define resources, steps, and expected results.

Acquiring data from the Web – web scraping tasks

Given the advances in the **Internet of Things (IoT)** and the progress of cloud computing, we can quietly affirm that in future, a huge part of our data will be available through the Internet, which on the other hand doesn't mean it will be public.

It is, therefore, crucial to know how to take that data from the Web and load it into your analytical environment.

You can find data on the Web either in the form of data statically stored on websites (that is, tables on Wikipedia or similar websites) or in the form of data stored on the cloud, which is accessible via APIs.

For API recipes, we will go through all the steps you need to get data statically exposed on websites in the form of tabular and nontabular data.

This specific example will show you how to get data from a specific Wikipedia page, the one about the R programming language: `https://en.wikipedia.org/wiki/R_ (programming_language)`.

Getting ready

Data statically exposed on web pages is actually pieces of web page code. Getting them from the Web to our R environment requires us to read that code and find where exactly the data is.

Dealing with complex web pages can become a really challenging task, but luckily, SelectorGadget was developed to help you with this job. SelectorGadget is a bookmarklet, developed by Andrew Cantino and Kyle Maxwell, that lets you easily figure out the CSS selector of your data on the web page you are looking at. Basically, the CSS selector can be seen as the address of your data on the web page, and you will need it within the R code that you are going to write to scrape your data from the Web (refer to the next paragraph).

> The CSS selector is the token that is used within the CSS code to identify elements of the HTML code based on their name.
>
> CSS selectors are used within the CSS code to identify which elements are to be styled using a given piece of CSS code. For instance, the following script will align all elements (CSS selector *) with 0 margin and 0 padding:
>
> ```
> * {
> margin: 0;
> padding: 0;
> }
> ```

SelectorGadget is currently employable only via the Chrome browser, so you will need to install the browser before carrying on with this recipe. You can download and install the last version of Chrome from `https://www.google.com/chrome/`.

SelectorGadget is available as a Chrome extension; navigate to the following URL while already on the page showing the data you need:

```
:javascript:(function(){
  var%20s=document.createElement('div');
  s.innerHTML='Loading...'
  ;s.style.color='black';
  s.style.padding='20px';
  s.style.position='fixed';
  s.style.zIndex='9999';
  s.style.fontSize='3.0em';
  s.style.border='2px%20solid%20black';
  s.style.right='40px';
  s.style.top='40px';
  s.setAttribute('class','selector_gadget_loading');
  s.style.background='white';
    document.body.appendChild(s);
```

```
s=document.createElement('script');
s.setAttribute('type','text/javascript');
s.setAttribute('src','https://dv0akt2986vzh.cloudfront.net/
unstable/lib/selectorgadget.js');document.body.appendChild(s);
})();
```

This long URL shows that the CSS selector is provided as JavaScript; you can make this out from the `:javascript:` token at the very beginning.

We can further analyze the URL by decomposing it into three main parts, which are as follows:

▸ Creation on the page of a new element of the `div` class with the `document.createElement('div')` statement

▸ Aesthetic attributes setting, composed by all the `s.style...` tokens

▸ The `.js` file content retrieving at `https://dv0akt2986vzh.cloudfront.net/unstable/lib/selectorgadget.js`

The `.js` file is where the CSS selector's core functionalities are actually defined and the place where they are taken to make them available to users.

That being said, I'm not suggesting that you try to use this link to employ SelectorGadget for your web scraping purposes, but I would rather suggest that you look for the Chrome extension or at the official SelectorGadget page, `http://selectorgadget.com`. Once you find the link on the official page, save it as a bookmark so that it is easily available when you need it.

The other tool we are going to use in this recipe is the `rvest` package, which offers great web scraping functionalities within the R environment.

To make it available, you first have to install and load it in the global environment that runs the following:

```
install.packages("rvest")
library(rvest)
```

How to do it...

1. Run SelectorGadget. To do so, after navigating to the web page you are interested in, activate SelectorGadget by running the Chrome extension or clicking on the bookmark that we previously saved.

   In both cases, after activating the gadget, a **Loading...** message will appear, and then, you will find a bar on the bottom-right corner of your web browser, as shown in the following screenshot:

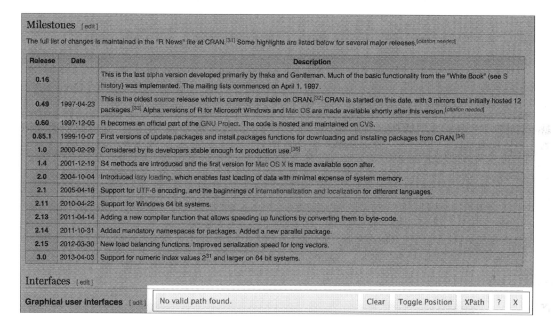

Milestones [edit]

The full list of changes is maintained in the "R News" file at CRAN.[31] Some highlights are listed below for several major releases.[citation needed]

Release	Date	Description
0.16		This is the last alpha version developed primarily by Ihaka and Gentleman. Much of the basic functionality from the "White Book" (see S history) was implemented. The mailing lists commenced on April 1, 1997.
0.49	1997-04-23	This is the oldest source release which is currently available on CRAN.[32] CRAN is started on this date, with 3 mirrors that initially hosted 12 packages.[33] Alpha versions of R for Microsoft Windows and Mac OS are made available shortly after this version.[citation needed]
0.60	1997-12-05	R becomes an official part of the GNU Project. The code is hosted and maintained on CVS.
0.65.1	1999-10-07	First versions of update.packages and install.packages functions for downloading and installing packages from CRAN.[34]
1.0	2000-02-29	Considered by its developers stable enough for production use.[35]
1.4	2001-12-19	S4 methods are introduced and the first version for Mac OS X is made available soon after.
2.0	2004-10-04	Introduced lazy loading, which enables fast loading of data with minimal expense of system memory.
2.1	2005-04-18	Support for UTF-8 encoding, and the beginnings of internationalization and localization for different languages.
2.11	2010-04-22	Support for Windows 64 bit systems.
2.13	2011-04-14	Adding a new compiler function that allows speeding up functions by converting them to byte-code.
2.14	2011-10-31	Added mandatory namespaces for packages. Added a new parallel package.
2.15	2012-03-30	New load balancing functions. Improved serialization speed for long vectors.
3.0	2013-04-03	Support for numeric index values 2^{31} and larger on 64 bit systems.

Interfaces [edit]

Graphical user interfaces [edit] | No valid path found. | Clear | Toggle Position | XPath | ? | X

You are now ready to select the data you are interested in.

2. Select the data you are interested in. After clicking on the data you are going to scrape, you will note that beside the data you've selected, there are some other parts on the page that will turn yellow:

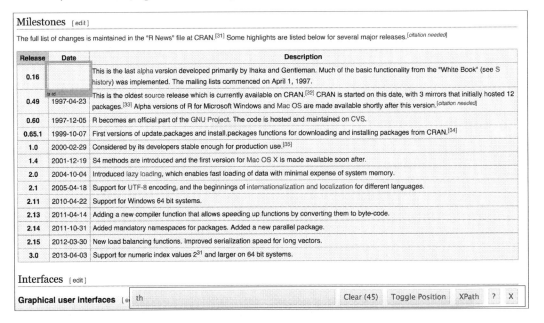

This is because SelectorGadget is trying to guess what you are looking at by highlighting all the elements included in the CSS selector that it considers to be most useful for you.

If it is guessing wrong, you just have to click on the wrongly highlighted parts and those will turn red:

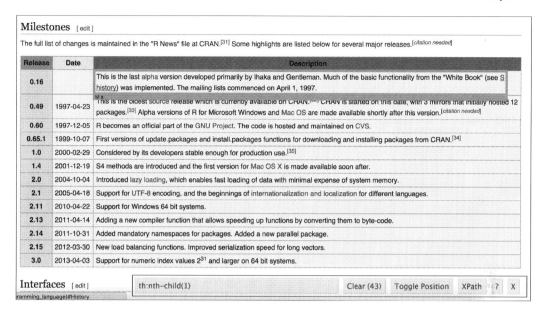

When you are done with this fine-tuning process, SelectorGadget will have correctly identified a proper selector, and you can move on to the next step.

3. Find your data location on the page. To do this, all you have to do is copy the CSS selector that you will find in the bar at the bottom-right corner:

This piece of text will be all you need in order to scrape the web page from R.

4. The next step is to read data from the Web with the `rvest` package. The `rvest` package by Hadley Wickham is one of the most comprehensive packages for web scraping activities in R. Take a look at the *There's more...* section for further information on package objectives and functionalities.

   For now, it is enough to know that the `rvest` package lets you download HTML code and read the data stored within the code easily.

   Now, we need to import the HTML code from the web page. First of all, we need to define an object storing all the HTML code of the web page you are looking at:

   ```
   page_source <-  read_html('https://en.wikipedia.org/wiki/R_
   (programming_language)
   ```

   This code leverages `read_html function()`, which retrieves the source code that resides at the written URL directly from the Web.

5. Next, we will select the defined blocks. Once you have got your HTML code, it is time to extract the part of the code you are interested in. This is done using the `html_nodes()` function, which is passed as an argument in the CSS selector and retrieved using SelectorGadget. This will result in a line of code similar to the following:

```
version_block    <- html_nodes(page_source,".wikitable th ,
.wikitable td")
```

As you can imagine, this code extracts all the content of the selected nodes, including HTML tags.

The HTML language

HyperText Markup Language (**HTML**) is a markup language that is used to define the format of web pages.

The basic idea behind HTML is to structure the web page into a format with a head and body, each of which contains a variable number of tags, which can be considered as subcomponents of the structure.

The head is used to store information and components that will not be seen by the user but will affect the web page's behavior, for instance, in a Google Analytics script used for tracking page visits, the body contains all the contents which will be showed to the reader.

Since the HTML code is composed of a nested structure, it is common to compare this structure to a tree, and here, different components are also referred to as nodes.

Printing out the `version_block` object, you will obtain a result similar to the following:

```
print(version_block)

{xml_nodeset (45)}
 [1] <th>Release</th>
 [2] <th>Date</th>
 [3] <th>Description</th>
 [4] <th>0.16</th>
 [5] <td/>
 [6] <td>This is the last <a href="/wiki/Alpha_test" title="Alpha
test" class="mw-redirect">alp ...
 [7] <th>0.49</th>
 [8] <td style="white-space:nowrap;">1997-04-23</td>
 [9] <td>This is the oldest available <a href="/wiki/Source_code"
title="Source code">source</a ...
[10] <th>0.60</th>
[11] <td>1997-12-05</td>
[12] <td>R becomes an official part of the <a href="/wiki/GNU_
Project" title="GNU Project">GNU  ...
```

```
[13]  <th>1.0</th>
[14]  <td>2000-02-29</td>
[15]  <td>Considered by its developers stable enough for production
use.<sup id="cite_ref-35" cl ...
[16]  <th>1.4</th>
[17]  <td>2001-12-19</td>
[18]  <td>S4 methods are introduced and the first version for <a
href="/wiki/Mac_OS_X" title="Ma ...
[19]  <th>2.0</th>
[20]  <td>2004-10-04</td>
```

This result is not exactly what you are looking for if you are going to work with this data. However, you don't have to worry about that since we are going to give your text a better shape in the very next step.

6. In order to obtain a readable and actionable format, we need one more step: extracting text from HTML tags.

    This can be done using the `html_text()` function, which will result in a list containing all the text present within the HTML tags:

    ```
    content <- html_text(version_block)
    ```

    The final result will be a perfectly workable chunk of text containing the data needed for our analysis:

```
[1]  "Release"

[2]  "Date"

[3]  "Description"

[4]  "0.16"

[5]  ""

[6]  "This is the last alpha version developed primarily by
Ihaka and Gentleman. Much of the basic functionality from the
\"White Book\" (see S history) was implemented. The mailing lists
commenced on April 1, 1997."
[7]  "0.49"

[8]  "1997-04-23"

[9]  "This is the oldest available source release, and compiles
on a limited number of Unix-like platforms. CRAN is started on
this date, with 3 mirrors that initially hosted 12 packages. Alpha
versions of R for Microsoft Windows and Mac OS are made available
shortly after this version."
```

[10] "0.60"

[11] "1997-12-05"

[12] "R becomes an official part of the GNU
Project. The code is hosted and maintained on CVS."

[13] "1.0"

[14] "2000-02-29"

[15] "Considered by its developers
stable enough for production use.[35]"

[16] "1.4"

[17] "2001-12-19"

[18] "S4 methods are introduced and the first
version for Mac OS X is made available soon after."

[19] "2.0"

[20] "2004-10-04"

[21] "Introduced lazy loading, which enables fast
loading of data with minimal expense of system memory."

[22] "2.1"

[23] "2005-04-18"

[24] "Support for UTF-8 encoding, and the beginnings of
internationalization and localization for different languages."

[25] "2.11"

[26] "2010-04-22"

[27] "Support for Windows 64 bit systems."

[28] "2.13"

[29] "2011-04-14"

[30] "Adding a new compiler function that allows
speeding up functions by converting them to byte-code."

```
[31]  "2.14"

[32]  "2011-10-31"

[33]  "Added mandatory namespaces for
packages. Added a new parallel package."

[34]  "2.15"

[35]  "2012-03-30"

[36]  "New load balancing functions. Improved
serialization speed for long vectors."

[37]  "3.0"

[38]  "2013-04-03"

[39]  "Support for numeric index values
231 and larger on 64 bit systems."

[40]  "3.1"

[41]  "2014-04-10"

[42]  ""

[43]  "3.2"

[44]  "2015-04-16"

[45]  ""
```

There's more...

The following are a few useful resources that will help you get the most out of this recipe:

- ▸ A useful list of HTML tags, to show you how HTML files are structured and how to identify code that you need to get from these files, is provided at http://www.w3schools.com/tags/tag_code.asp
- ▸ The blog post from the RStudio guys introducing the rvest package and highlighting some package functionalities can be found at http://blog.rstudio.org/2014/11/24/rvest-easy-web-scraping-with-r/

Accessing an API with R

As we mentioned before, an always increasing proportion of our data resides on the Web and is made available through web APIs.

APIs in computer programming are intended to be APIs, groups of procedures, protocols, and software used for software application building. APIs expose software in terms of input, output, and processes.

Web APIs are developed as an interface between web applications and third parties.

The typical structure of a web API is composed of a set of HTTP request messages that have answers with a predefined structure, usually in the XML or JSON format.

A typical use case for API data contains data regarding web and mobile applications, for instance, Google Analytics data or data regarding social networking activities.

The successful web application **If This ThenThat** (**IFTTT**), for instance, lets you link together different applications, making them share data with each other and building powerful and customizable workflows:

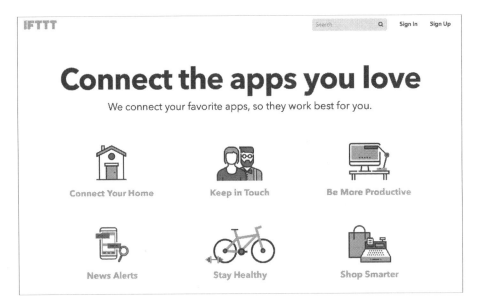

This useful job is done by leveraging the application's API (if you don't know IFTTT, just navigate to `https://ifttt.com`, and I will see you there).

Using R, it is possible to authenticate and get data from every API that adheres to the OAuth 1 and OAuth 2 standards, which are nowadays the most popular standards (even though opinions about these protocols are changing; refer to this popular post by the OAuth creator Blain Cook at `http://hueniverse.com/2012/07/26/oauth-2-0-and-the-road-to-hell/`). Moreover, specific packages have been developed for a lot of APIs.

This recipe shows how to access custom APIs and leverage packages developed for specific APIs.

In the *There's more...* section, suggestions are given on how to develop custom functions for frequently used APIs.

Getting ready

The `rvest` package, once again a product of our benefactor Hadley Whickham, provides a complete set of functionalities for sending and receiving data through the HTTP protocol on the Web. Take a look at the quick-start guide hosted on GitHub to get a feeling of `rvest` functionalities (`https://github.com/hadley/rvest`).

Among those functionalities, functions for dealing with APIs are provided as well.

Both OAuth 1.0 and OAuth 2.0 interfaces are implemented, making this package really useful when working with APIs.

Let's look at how to get data from the GitHub API. By changing small sections, I will point out how you can apply it to whatever API you are interested in.

Let's now actually install the `rvest` package:

```
install.packages("rvest")
library(rvest)
```

How to do it...

1. The first step to connect with the API is to define the API endpoint. Specifications for the endpoint are usually given within the API documentation. For instance, GitHub gives this kind of information at `http://developer.github.com/v3/oauth/`.

   In order to set the endpoint information, we are going to use the `oauth_endpoint()` function, which requires us to set the following arguments:

   - `request`: This is the URL that is required for the initial unauthenticated token. This is deprecated for OAuth 2.0, so you can leave it `NULL` in this case, since the GitHub API is based on this protocol.

   - `authorize`: This is the URL where it is possible to gain authorization for the given client.

> ❑ `access`: This is the URL where the exchange for an authenticated token is made.
>
> ❑ `base_url`: This is the API URL on which other URLs (that is, the URLs containing requests for data) will be built upon.

In the GitHub example, this will translate to the following line of code:

```
github_api <- oauth_endpoint(request    = NULL,
                             authorize =
"https://github.com/login/oauth/authorize",
        access   = "https://github.com/login/oauth/access_token",
                             base_url  =
"https://github.com/login/oauth")
```

2. Create an application to get a key and secret token. Moving on with our GitHub example, in order to create an application, you will have to navigate to `https://github.com/settings/applications/new` (assuming that you are already authenticated on GitHub).

    Be aware that no particular URL is needed as the homepage URL, but a specific URL is required as the authorization callback URL.

    This is the URL that the API will redirect to after the method invocation is done.

    As you would expect, since we want to establish a connection from GitHub to our local PC, you will have to redirect the API to your machine, setting the Authorization callback URL to `http://localhost:1410`.

    After creating your application, you can get back to your R session to establish a connection with it and get your data.

3. After getting back to your R session, you now have to set your OAuth credentials through the `oaut_app()` and `oauth2.0_token()` functions and establish a connection with the API, as shown in the following code snippet:

```
app <- oauth_app("your_app_name",
  key = "your_app_key",
  secret = "your_app_secret")
  API_token <- oauth2.0_token(github_api,app)
```

4. This is where you actually use the API to get data from your web-based software. Continuing on with our GitHub-based example, let's request some information about API rate limits:

```
request <- GET("https://api.github.com/rate_limit", config(token =
API_token))
```

How it works...

Be aware that this step will be required both for OAuth 1.0 and OAuth 2.0 APIs, as the difference between them is only the absence of a request URL, as we noted earlier.

Endpoints for popular APIs

The `httr` package comes with a set of endpoints that are already implemented for popular APIs, and specifically for the following websites:

- LinkedIn
- Twitter
- Vimeo
- Google
- Facebook
- GitHub

For these APIs, you can substitute the call to `oauth_endpoint()` with a call to the `oauth_endpoints()` function, for instance:

```
oauth_endpoints("github")
```

 The core feature of the OAuth protocol is to secure authentication. This is then provided on the client side through a key and secret token, which are to be kept private.

The typical way to get a key and a secret token to access an API involves creating an app within the service providing the API.

The callback URL

Within the web API domain, a callback URL is the URL that is called by the API after the answer is given to the request. A typical example of a callback URL is the URL of the page navigated to after completing an online purchase.

In this example, when we finish at the checkout on the online store, an API call is made to the payment circuit provider.

After completing the payment operation, the API will navigate again to the online store at the callback URL, usually to a thank you page.

There's more...

You can also write custom functions to handle APIs. When frequently dealing with a particular API, it can be useful to define a set of custom functions in order to make it easier to interact with.

Basically, the interaction with an API can be summarized with the following three categories:

- ▶ Authentication
- ▶ Getting content from the API
- ▶ Posting content to the API

Authentication can be handled by leveraging the HTTR package's `authenticate()` function and writing a function as follows:

```
api_auth    function (path = "api_path", password){
authenticate(user = path, password)
}
```

You can get the content from the API through the `get` function of the `httr` package:

```
api_get <- function(path = "api_path",password){
auth <- api_auth(path, password )
request <- GET("https://api.com", path = path, auth)

}
```

Posting content will be done in a similar way through the POST function:

```
api_post <- function(Path, post_body, path = "api_path",password){
auth <- api_auth(pat) stopifnot(is.list(body))
body_json <- jsonlite::toJSON(body)
request <- POST("https://api.application.com", path = path, body =
body_json, auth, post, ...)
}
```

Getting data from Twitter with the twitteR package

Twitter is an unbeatable source of data for nearly every kind of data-driven problem.

If my words are not enough to convince you, and I think they shouldn't be, you can always perform a quick search on Google, for instance, *text analytics with Twitter*, and read the over 30 million results to be sure.

This should not surprise you, given Google's huge and word-spreaded base of users together with the relative structure and richness of metadata of content on the platform, which makes this social network a place to go when talking about data analysis projects, especially those involving sentiment analysis and customer segmentations.

R comes with a really well-developed package named `twitteR`, developed by Jeff Gentry, which offers a function for nearly every functionality made available by Twitter through the API. The following recipe covers the typical use of the package: getting tweets related to a topic.

Getting ready

First of all, we have to install our great `twitteR` package by running the following code:

```
install.packages("twitteR")
library(twitter)
```

How to do it...

1. As seen with the general procedure, in order to access the Twitter API, you will need to create a new application. This link (assuming you are already logged in to Twitter) will do the job: `https://apps.twitter.com/app/new`.

    Feel free to give whatever name, description, and website to your app that you want. The callback URL can be also left blank.

    After creating the app, you will have access to an API key and an API secret, namely **Consumer Key** and **Consumer Secret**, in the **Keys and Access Tokens** tab in your app settings.

    Below the section containing these tokens, you will find a section called **Your Access Token**. These tokens are required in order to let the app perform actions on your account's behalf. For instance, you may be willing to send direct messages to all new followers and could therefore write an app to do that automatically.

    Keep a note of these tokens as well, since you will need them to set up your connection within R.

2. Then, we will get access to the API from R. In order to authenticate your app and use it to retrieve data from Twitter, you will just need to run a line of code, specifically, the `setup_twitter_oauth()` function, by passing the following arguments:

    ❑   `consumer_key`

    ❑   `consumer_token`

    ❑   `access_token`

    ❑   `access_secret`

    You can get these tokens from your app settings:

    ```
    setup_twitter_oauth(consumer_key     = "consumer_key",
                        consumer_secret  = "consumer_secret",
                        access_token     = "access_token",
                        access_secret    = "access_secret")
    ```

3. Now, we will query Twitter and store the resulting data. We are finally ready for the core part: getting data from Twitter. Since we are looking for tweets pertaining to a specific topic, we are going to use the `searchTwitter()` function. This function allows you to specify a good number of parameters besides the search string. You can define the following:

- `n` : This is the number of tweets to be downloaded.

- `lang`: This is the language specified with the ISO 639-1 code. You can find a partial list of this code at `https://en.wikipedia.org/wiki/List_of_ISO_639-1_codes`.

- `since` – `until`: These are time parameters that define a range of time, where dates are expressed as YYYY-MM-DD, for instance, 2012-05-12.

- `locale`: This specifies the geocode, expressed as latitude, longitude and radius, either in miles or kilometers, for example, 38.481157, -130.500342,1 mi.

- `sinceID` – `maxID`: This is the account ID range.

- `resultType`: This is used to filter results based on popularity. Possible values are 'mixed', 'recent', and 'popular'.

- `retryOnRateLimit`: This is the number that defines how many times the query will be retried if the API rate limit is reached.

Supposing that we are interested in tweets regarding data science with R; we run the following function:

```
tweet_list <- searchTwitter('data science with R', n = 450)
```

Performing a character-wise search with twitteR

Searching Twitter for a specific sequence of characters is possible by submitting a query surrounded by double quotes, for instance, `"data science with R"`. Consequently, if you are looking to retrieve tweets in R corresponding to a specific sequence of characters, you will have to submit and run a line of code similar to the following:

```
tweet_list <- searchTwitter('data science with R', n = 450)
```

`tweet_list` will be a list of the first 450 tweets resulting from the given query.

Be aware that since n is the maximum number of tweets retrievable, you may retrieve a smaller number of tweets, if for the given query the number or result is smaller than n.

Each element of the list will show the following attributes:

- text
- favorited
- favoriteCount
- replyToSN
- created
- truncated
- replyToSID
- id
- replyToUID
- statusSource
- screenName
- retweetCount
- isRetweet
- retweeted
- longitude
- latitude

In order to let you work on this data more easily, a specific function is provided to transform this list in a more convenient `data.frame`, namely, the `twiLstToDF()` function.

After this, we can run the following line of code:

```
tweet_df   <-   twListToDF(tweet_list)
```

This will result in a `tweet_df` object that has the following structure:

```
> str(tweet_df)
'data.frame':   20 obs. of   16 variables:
 $ text          : chr  "95% off  Applied Data Science with R -
 $ favorited     : logi  FALSE FALSE FALSE FALSE FALSE FALSE ...
 $ favoriteCount : num  0 2 0 2 0 0 0 0 0 1 ...
 $ replyToSN     : logi  NA NA NA NA NA NA ...
 $ created       : POSIXct, format: "2015-10-16 09:03:32" "2015-10-
15 17:40:33" "2015-10-15 11:33:37" "2015-10-15 05:17:59" ...
 $ truncated     : logi  FALSE FALSE FALSE FALSE FALSE FALSE ...
 $ replyToSID    : logi  NA NA NA NA NA NA ...
 $ id            : chr  "654945762384740352" "654713487097135104"
"654621142179819520" "654526612688375808" ...
 $ replyToUID    : logi  NA NA NA NA NA NA ...
```

```
$ statusSource : chr  "<a href=\"http://learnviral.com/\"
rel=\"nofollow\">Learn Viral</a>" "<a href=\"https://about.
twitter.com/products/tweetdeck\" rel=\"nofollow\">TweetDeck</
a>" "<a href=\"http://not.yet/\" rel=\"nofollow\">final one kk</
a>" "<a href=\"http://twitter.com\" rel=\"nofollow\">Twitter Web
Client</a>" ...
$ screenName    : chr  "Learn_Viral" "WinVectorLLC" "retweetjava"
"verystrongjoe" ...
$ retweetCount  : num  0 0 1 1 0 0 0 2 2 2 ...
$ isRetweet     : logi  FALSE FALSE TRUE FALSE FALSE FALSE ...
$ retweeted     : logi  FALSE FALSE FALSE FALSE FALSE FALSE ...
$ longitude     : logi  NA NA NA NA NA NA ...
$ latitude      : logi  NA NA NA NA NA NA ...
```

After sending you to the data visualization section for advanced techniques, we will now quickly visualize the retweet distribution of our tweets, leveraging the base R `hist()` function:

```
hist(tweet_df$retweetCount)
```

This code will result in a histogram that has the x axis as the number of retweets and the y axis as the frequency of those numbers:

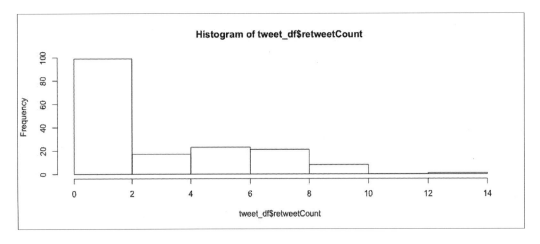

There's more...

As stated in the official Twitter documentation, particularly at `https://dev.twitter.com/rest/public/rate-limits`, there is a limit to the number of tweets you can retrieve within a certain period of time, and this limit is set to 450 every 15 minutes.

However, what if you are engaged in a really sensible job and you want to base your work on a significant number of tweets? Should you set the n argument of `searchTwitter()` to 450 and wait for 15—everlasting—minutes? Not quite, the `twitteR` package provides a convenient way to overcome this limit through the `register_db_backend()`, `register_sqlite_backend()`, and `register_mysql_bakend()` functions. These functions allow you to create a connection with the named type of databases, passing the database name, path, username, and password as arguments, as you can see in the following example:

```
register_mysql_backend("db_name", "host","user","password")
```

You can now leverage the `search_twitter_and_store` function, which stores the search results in the connected database. The main feature of this function is the `retryOnRateLimit` argument, which lets you specify the number of tries to be performed by the code once the API limit is reached. Setting this limit to a convenient level will likely let you pass the 15-minutes interval:

```
tweets_db = search_twitter_and_store("data science R",
retryOnRateLimit = 20)
```

Retrieving stored data will now just require you to run the following code:

```
from_db = load_tweets_db()
```

Getting data from Facebook with the Rfacebook package

The Rfacebook package, developed and maintained by Pablo Barberá, lets you easily establish and take advantage of Facebook's API thanks to a series of functions.

As we did for the twitteR package, we are going to establish a connection with the API and retrieve posts pertaining to a given keyword.

Getting ready

This recipe will mainly be based on functions from the Rfacebok package. Therefore, we need to install and load this package in our environment:

```
install.packages("Rfacebook")
library(Rfacebook)
```

How to do it...

1. In order to leverage an API's functionalities, we first have to create an application in our Facebook profile. Navigating to the following URL will let you create an app (assuming you are already logged in to Facebook): `https://developers.facebook.com`.

   After skipping the quick start (the button on the upper-right corner), you can see the settings of your app and take note of `app_id` and `app_secret`, which you will need in order to establish a connection with the app.

2. After installing and loading the Rfacebook package, you will easily be able to establish a connection by running the `fbOAuth()` function as follows:

   ```
   fb_connection <-   fbOauth(app_id       = "your_app_id",
                             app_secret = "your_app_secret")

   fb_connection
   ```

   Running the last line of code will result in a console prompt, as shown in the following lines of code:

   ```
   copy and paste into site URL on Facebook App Settings: http://
   localhost:1410/ When done press any key to continue
   ```

   Following this prompt, you will have to copy the URL and go to your Facebook app settings.

   Once there, you will have to select the **Settings** tab and create a new platform through the **+ Add Platform** control. In the form, which will prompt you after clicking this control, you should find a field named **Site Url**. In this field, you will have to paste the copied URL.

   Close the process by clicking on the **Save Changes** button.

   At this point, a browser window will open up and ask you to allow access permission from the app to your profile. After allowing this permission, the R console will print out the following code snippet:

   ```
   Authentication complete

   Authentication successful.
   ```

3. To test our API connection, we are going to search Facebook for posts related to data science with R and save the results within `data.frame` for further analysis.

   Among other useful functions, Rfacebook provides the `searchPages()` function, which as you would expect, allows you to search the social network for pages mentioning a given string.

Different from the `searchTwitter` function, this function will not let you specify a lot of arguments:

- `string`: This is the query string
- `token`: This is the valid OAuth token created with the `fbOAuth()` function
- `n`: This is the maximum number of posts to be retrieved

The Unix timestamp

The Unix timestamp is a time-tracking system originally developed for the Unix OS. Technically, the Unix timestamp x expresses the number of seconds elapsed since the Unix Epoch (January 1, 1970 UTC) and the timestamp.

To search for data science with R, you will have to run the following line of code:

```
pages ← searchPages('data science with R',fb_connection)
```

This will result in `data.frame` storing all the pages retrieved along with the data concerning them.

As seen for the twitteR package, we can take a quick look at the like distribution, leveraging the base R `hist()` function:

```
hist(pages$likes)
```

This will result in a plot similar to the following:

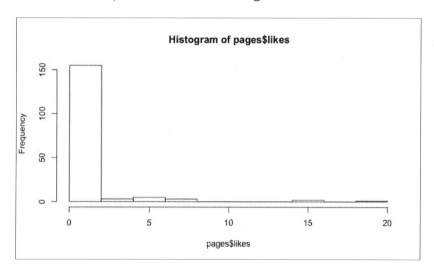

Refer to the data visualization section for further recipes on data visualization.

Getting data from Google Analytics

Google Analytics is a powerful analytics solution that gives you really detailed insights into how your online content is performing. However, besides a tabular format and a data visualization tool, no other instruments are available to model your data and gain more powerful insights.

This is where R comes to help, and this is why the `RGoogleAnalytics` package was developed: to provide a convenient way to extract data from Google Analytics into an R environment.

As an example, we will import data from Google Analytics into R regarding the daily bounce rate for a website in a given time range.

Getting ready

As a preliminary step, we are going to install and load the `RGoogleAnalytics` package:

```
install.packages("RGoogeAnalytics")
library(RGoogleAnalytics)
```

How to do it...

1. The first step that is required to get data from Google Analytics is to create a Google Analytics application.

   This can be easily obtained from (assuming that you are already logged in to Google Analytics) `https://console.developers.google.com/apis`.

   After creating a new project, you will see a dashboard with a left menu containing among others the **APIs & auth** section, with the **APIs** subsection.

   After selecting this section, you will see a list of available APIs, and among these, at the bottom-left corner of the page, there will be the **Advertising APIs** with the **Analytics API** within it:

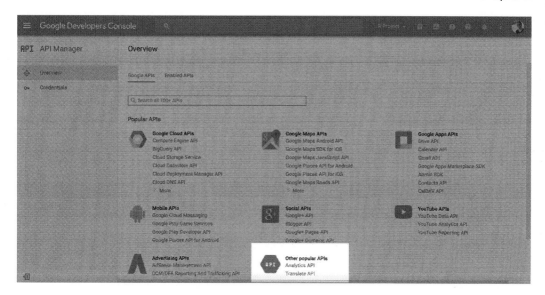

After enabling the API, you will have to go back to the **APIs & auth** section and select the **Credentials** subsection.

In this section, you will have to add an **OAuth client ID**, select **Other**, and assign a name to your app:

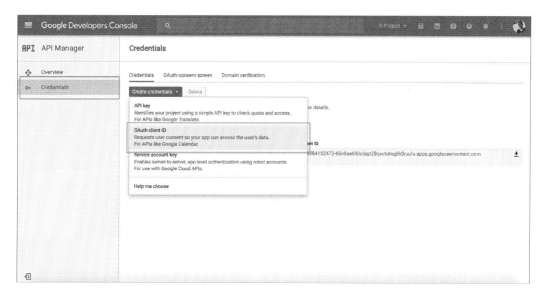

After doing that and selecting the **Create** button, you will be prompted with a window showing your app ID and secret. Take note of them, as you will need them to access the analytics API from R.

2. In order to authenticate on the API, we will leverage the `Auth()` function, providing the annotated ID and secret:

```
ga_token <- Auth(client.id = "the_ID", client.secret = "the_
secret")
```

At this point, a browser window will open up and ask you to allow access permission from the app to your Google Analytics account.

After you allow access, the R console will print out the following:

```
Authentication complete
```

3. This last step basically requires you to shape a proper query and submit it through the connection established in the previous paragraphs. A Google Analytics query can be easily built, leveraging the powerful Google Query explorer which can be found at `https://ga-dev-tools.appspot.com/query-explorer/`.

This web tool lets you experiment with query parameters and define your query before submitting the request from your code.

The basic fields that are mandatory in order to execute a query are as follows:

-   **The view ID**: This is a unique identifier associated with your Google Analytics property. This ID will automatically show up within Google Query Explorer.

-   **Start-date and end-date**: This is the start and end date in the form YYYY-MM-DD, for example, 2012-05-12.

-   **Metrics**: This refers to the ratios and numbers computed from the data related to visits within the date range. You can find the metrics code in Google Query Explorer.

If you are going to further elaborate your data within your data project, you will probably find it useful to add a date dimension (`"ga:date"`) in order to split your data by date.

Having defined your arguments, you will just have to pack them in a list using the `init()` function, build a query using the `QueryBuilder()` function, and submit it with the `GetReportData()` function:

```
query_parameters <- Init(start.date = "2015-01-01",
                         end.date   = "2015-06-30",
                         metrics    =   "ga:sessions,
                                         ga:bounceRate",
                         dimensions = "ga:date",
                         table.id = "ga:33093633")
ga_query <- QueryBuilder(query_parameters)
ga_df <- GetReportData(ga_query, ga_token)
```

The first representation of this data could be a simple plot of data that will result in a representation of the bounce rate for each day from the start date to the end date:

```
plot(ga_df)
```

There's more...

Google Analytics is a complete and always-growing set of tools for performing web analytics tasks. If you are facing a project involving the use of this platform, I would definitely suggest that you take the time to go through the official tutorial from Google at `https://analyticsacademy.withgoogle.com`.

This complete set of tutorials will introduce you to the fundamental logic and assumptions of the platform, giving you a solid foundation for any of the following analysis.

Loading your data into R with rio packages

The `rio` package is a relatively recent R package, developed by Thomas J. Leeper, which makes data import and export in R painless and quick.

This objective is mainly reached when *rio* makes assumptions about the file format. This means that the *rio* package guesses the format of the file you are trying to import and consequently applies import functions appropriate to that format.

All of this is done behind the scenes, and the user is just required to run the `import()` function.

As Leeper often states when talking about the package: "it just works."

One of the great results you can obtain by employing this package is streamlining workflows involving different development and productivity tools.

For instance, it is possible to produce tables directly into SAS and make them available to the R environment without any particular export procedure in SAS, we can directly acquire data in R as it is produced, or input into an Excel spreadsheet.

Getting ready

As you would expect, we first need to install and load the `rio` package:

```
install.packages("rio")
library(rio)
```

In the following example, we are going to import our well-known `world_gdp_data` dataset from a local `.csv` file.

How to do it...

1. The first step is to import the dataset using the `import()` function:

   ```
   messy_gdp ← import("world_gdp_data.csv")
   ```

2. Then, we visualize the result with the RStudio viewer:

   ```
   View(messy_gdp)
   ```

How it works...

We first import the dataset using the `import()` function. To understand the structure of the `import()` function, we can leverage a useful behavior of the R console: putting a function name without parentheses and running the command will result in the printing of all the function definitions.

Running the import on the R console will produce the following output:

```
function (file, format, setclass, ...)
{
    if (missing(format))
        fmt <- get_ext(file)
    else fmt <- tolower(format)
    if (grepl("^http.*://", file)) {
        temp_file <- tempfile(fileext = fmt)
        on.exit(unlink(temp_file))
        curl_download(file, temp_file, mode = "wb")
        file <- temp_file
    }
    x <- switch(fmt, r = dget(file = file), tsv = import.delim(file =
file,
        sep = "\t", ...), txt = import.delim(file = file, sep = "\t",
        ...), fwf = import.fwf(file = file, ...), rds = readRDS(file =
file,
        ...), csv = import.delim(file = file, sep = ",", ...),
        csv2 = import.delim(file = file, sep = ";", dec = ",",
        ...), psv = import.delim(file = file, sep = "|",
        ...), rdata = import.rdata(file = file, ...), dta =
import.dta(file = file,
        ...), dbf = read.dbf(file = file, ...), dif = read.
DIF(file = file,
        ...), sav = import.sav(file = file, ...), por = read_
por(path = file),
        sas7bdat = read_sas(b7dat = file, ...), xpt = read.xport(file
= file),
```

```
           mtp = read.mtp(file = file, ...), syd = read.systat(file =
       file,
                   to.data.frame = TRUE), json = fromJSON(txt = file,
                   ...), rec = read.epiinfo(file = file, ...), arff = read.
       arff(file = file),
               xls = read_excel(path = file, ...), xlsx = import.xlsx(file =
       file,
                   ...), fortran = import.fortran(file = file, ...),
               zip = import.zip(file = file, ...), tar = import.tar(file =
       file,
                   ...), ods = import.ods(file = file, ...), xml = import.
       xml(file = file,
                   ...), clipboard = import.clipboard(...), gnumeric =
       stop(stop_for_import(fmt)),
               jpg = stop(stop_for_import(fmt)), png = stop(stop_for_
       import(fmt)),
               bmp = stop(stop_for_import(fmt)), tiff = stop(stop_for_
       import(fmt)),
               sss = stop(stop_for_import(fmt)), sdmx = stop(stop_for_
       import(fmt)),
               matlab = stop(stop_for_import(fmt)), gexf = stop(stop_for_
       import(fmt)),
               npy = stop(stop_for_import(fmt)), stop("Unrecognized file
       format"))
       if (missing(setclass)) {
           return(set_class(x))
       }
       else {
           a <- list(...)
           if ("data.table" %in% names(a) && isTRUE(a[["data.table"]]))
               setclass <- "data.table"
           return(set_class(x, class = setclass))
       }
   }
```

As you can see, the first task performed by the import() function calls the get_ext() function, which basically retrieves the extension from the filename.

Once the file format is clear, the import() function looks for the right subimport function to be used and returns the result of this function.

Next, we visualize the result with the RStudio viewer. One of the most powerful RStudio tools is the data viewer, which lets you get a spreadsheet-like view of your data.frame objects. With RStudio 0.99, this tool got even more powerful, removing the previous 1000-row limit and adding the ability to filter and format your data in the correct order.

When using this viewer, you should be aware that all filtering and ordering activities will not affect the original data.frame object you are visualizing.

There's more...

As fully illustrated within the Rio vignette (which can be found at `https://cran.r-project.org/web/packages/rio/vignettes/rio.html`), the following formats are supported for import and export:

Format	Import	Export
Tab-separated data (`.tsv`)	Yes	Yes
Comma-separated data (`.csv`)	Yes	Yes
CSVY (CSV + YAML metadata header) (`.csvy`)	Yes	Yes
Pipe-separated data (`.psv`)	Yes	Yes
Fixed-width format data (`.fwf`)	Yes	Yes
Serialized R objects (`.rds`)	Yes	Yes
Saved R objects (`.RData`)	Yes	Yes
JSON (`.json`)	Yes	Yes
YAML (`.yml`)	Yes	Yes
Stata (`.dta`)	Yes	Yes
SPSS and SPSS portable	Yes (`.sav` and `.por`)	Yes (`.sav` only)
XBASE database files (`.dbf`)	Yes	Yes
Excel (`.xls`)	Yes	
Excel (`.xlsx`)	Yes	Yes
Weka Attribute-Relation File Format (`.arff`)	Yes	Yes
R syntax (`.R`)	Yes	Yes
Shallow XML documents (`.xml`)	Yes	Yes
SAS (`.sas7bdat`)	Yes	
SAS XPORT (`.xpt`)	Yes	
Minitab (`.mtp`)	Yes	
Epiinfo (`.rec`)	Yes	
Systat (`.syd`)	Yes	
Data Interchange Format (`.dif`)	Yes	
OpenDocument Spreadsheet (`.ods`)	Yes	
Fortran data (no recognized extension)	Yes	
Google Sheets	Yes	
Clipboard (default is `.tsv`)		

Since Rio is still a growing package, I strongly suggest that you follow its development on its GitHub repository, where you will easily find out when new formats are added, at `https://github.com/leeper/rio`.

Converting file formats using the rio package

As we saw in the previous recipe, Rio is an R package developed by Thomas J. Leeper which makes the import and export of data really easy. You can refer to the previous recipe for more on its core functionalities and logic.

Besides the `import()` and `export()` functions, Rio also offers a really well-conceived and straightforward file conversion facility through the `convert()` function, which we are going to leverage in this recipe.

Getting ready

First of all, we need to install and make the `rio` package available by running the following code:

```
install.packages("rio")
library(rio)
```

In the following example, we are going to import the `world_gdp_data` dataset from a local `.csv` file. This dataset is provided within the RStudio project related to this book, in the `data` folder.

You can download it by authenticating your account at `http://packtpub.com`.

How to do it...

1. The first step is to convert the file from the `.csv` format to the `.json` format:

    ```
    convert("world_gdp_data.csv", "world_gdp_data.json")
    ```

    This will create a new file without removing the original one.

2. The next step is to remove the original file:

    ```
    file.remove("world_gdp_data.csv")
    ```

There's more...

As fully illustrated within the Rio vignette (which you can find at `https://cran.r-project.org/web/packages/rio/vignettes/rio.html`), the following formats are supported for import and export:

Format	Import	Export
Tab-separated data (`.tsv`)	Yes	Yes
Comma-separated data (`.csv`)	Yes	Yes
CSVY (CSV + YAML metadata header) (`.csvy`)	Yes	Yes
Pipe-separated data (`.psv`)	Yes	Yes
Fixed-width format data (`.fwf`)	Yes	Yes
Serialized R objects (`.rds`)	Yes	Yes
Saved R objects (`.RData`)	Yes	Yes
JSON (`.json`)	Yes	Yes
YAML (`.yml`)	Yes	Yes
Stata (`.dta`)	Yes	Yes
SPSS and SPSS portable	Yes (`.sav` and `.por`)	Yes (`.sav` only)
XBASE database files (`.dbf`)	Yes	Yes
Excel (`.xls`)	Yes	
Excel (`.xlsx`)	Yes	Yes
Weka Attribute-Relation File Format (`.arff`)	Yes	Yes
R syntax (`.r`)	Yes	Yes
Shallow XML documents (`.xml`)	Yes	Yes
SAS (`.sas7bdat`)	Yes	
SAS XPORT (`.xpt`)	Yes	
Minitab (`.mtp`)	Yes	
Epiinfo (`.rec`)	Yes	
Systat (`.syd`)	Yes	
Data Interchange Format (`.dif`)	Yes	
OpenDocument Spreadsheet (`.ods`)	Yes	
Fortran data (no recognized extension)	Yes	
Google Sheets	Yes	
Clipboard (default is `.tsv`)		

Since `rio` is still a growing package, I strongly suggest that you follow its development on its GitHub repository, where you will easily find out when new formats are added, at `https://github.com/leeper/rio`.

2

Preparing for Analysis – Data Cleansing and Manipulation

In this chapter, we will cover the following topics:

- ▶ Getting a sense of your data structure with R
- ▶ Preparing your data for analysis with the tidyr package
- ▶ Detecting missing values
- ▶ Substituting missing values by interpolation
- ▶ Detecting and removing outliers
- ▶ Performing data filtering activities

Introduction

Some studies estimate that data preparation activities account for 80 percent of the time invested in data science projects.

I know you will not be surprised reading this number. Data preparation is the phase in data science projects where you take your data from the chaotic world around you and fit it into some precise structures and standards.

This is absolutely not a simple task and involves a great number of techniques that basically let you change the structure of your data and ensure you can work with it.

This chapter will show you recipes that should give you the ability to prepare the data you got from the previous chapter, no matter how it was structured when you acquired it in R.

We will look at the two main activities performed during the data preparation phase:

- **Data cleansing**: This involves identification and treatment of outliers and missing values
- **Data manipulation**: Here, the main aim is to make the data structure fit some specific rule, which will let the user employ it for analysis

Getting a sense of your data structure with R

By following the recipes given in the previous chapter, you got your data. Everything went smoothly, and you may also already have the data as a data frame object.

However, do you know what your data looks like?

Getting to know your data structure is a crucial step within a data analysis project. It will suggest the appropriate treatment and analysis, and will help you avoid error and redundancy in the coding activity that follows.

In this recipe, we will look at a dataset structure by leveraging the `describe()` function from the `Hmisc` package. For further preliminary analysis on your data structure, you can also refer to the data visualization recipes in *Chapter 3, Basic Visualization Techniques*.

Getting ready

This example will be built around a dataset provided in the RStudio project related to this book.

You can download it by authenticating your account at `http://packtpub.com`.

This dataset is named `world_gdp_data.csv` and stores GDP values for 248 countries around the globe, from 1960 to 2015.

Before you begin with this recipe, you will need to load this data into R by leveraging the `import` function from the `rio` package:

```
install.packages("rio")
library(rio)
messy_gdp <- import("world_gdp_data.csv")
```

You can refer to the *Loading your data into R with rio packages* recipe in *Chapter 1, Acquiring Data for Your Project*, for details on this powerful tool's functionalities.

As mentioned earlier, we will employ functions from the `Hmisc` and `e1071` packages.

Use the following code to install and load packages:

```
install.packages(c("Hmisc","e1071"))
library(Hmisc)
library(e1071)
```

How to do it...

1. Create a data dictionary:

   ```
   data_dictionary <- describe(messy_gdp)
   ```

2. Save your data dictionary as a separate file to document it:

   ```
   sink("data_dictionary.txt", append=TRUE)
   data_dictionary
   sink()
   ```

3. Look at your data dictionary:

   ```
   file.show(file = "data_dictionary.txt",pager = "internal")
   ```

How it works...

Preforming step 1 will produce a `data_dictionary` object, which is a list of as many lists as there are columns in your data frame plus one, the contents of which we are going to discover lately.

For each column, the following details are exposed:

▸ Variability domain, showing the lowest and highest values

▸ Number of non-missing values

▸ Number of missing values

▸ Number of unique values

▸ For categorical variables (for instance, country names), a frequency table is produced, showing the number of occurrences for each possible value of the variable

The last list is populated only if the columns of all missing values are read and contain the name of those columns.

Step 2 lets you create a document to which you will be able to refer, even outside R, mainly for documentation purposes. This step will produce a `.txt` file named `data_dictionary` placed within the current directory of your R session.

Since the `data_dictionary` object is a `list` object, we can't simply save it as a `.txt` file (we could easily do this with the `write()` function when dealing with a data frame). So, we used a workaround involving the `sink()` function.

This function sends the output of R to an external connection.

The logical phases of this process are as follows:

1. Establish a connection by running `sink()` for the first time
2. Run the R code you are interested in
3. Close the connection by running `sink()` again

Step 3 is the final step and involves calling the `file.show` function to show you your previously created data dictionary. Be aware that changing the `pager` argument to `console` would make the `.txt` file content show up in the R console.

Preparing your data for analysis with the tidyr package

The `tidyr` package is another gift from Hadley Wickham. This package provides functions to make your data tidy.

This means that after applying the `tidyr` package's function, your data you will be arranged as per the following rules:

- Each column will contain an attribute
- Each row will contain an observation
- Each cell will contain a value

These rules will produce a dataset similar to the following one:

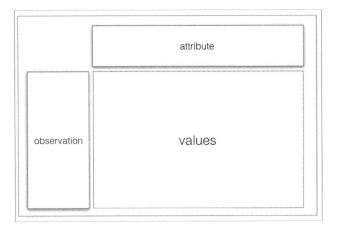

This structure, besides giving you a clearer understanding of your data, will let you work with it more easily.

Furthermore, this structure will let you take full advantage of the inner R-vectorized structure. This recipe will show you how to apply the `gather` function to a dataset in order to transform a dataset and make it comply with the cited rules.

The employed data frame is in the so-called **wide format**, where each period of observation is stored in columns, with each column representing a year, as follows:

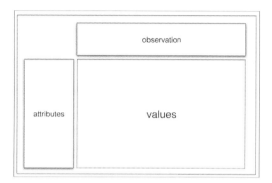

Getting ready

In order to let you apply the `tidyr` function, you will have to install and load the `tidyr` package within your R environment by running the following code:

```
install.packages("tidyr")
library(tidyr)
```

Moreover, we will need to install and load the `rio` package, which is covered in greater detail in the *Loading your data into R with rio packages* recipe in *Chapter 1, Acquiring Data for Your Project*:

```
install.packages("rio")
library(rio)
```

The dataset tidied in this recipe is the `world_gdp_data.csv` dataset.

This dataset is provided in the RStudio project for this book.

You can download it by authenticating your account at `http://packtpub.com`.

The `world_gdp_data` dataset stores GDP values for 248 countries around the globe, from 1960 to 2015.

In the *There's more…* section, you will find other examples of messy data for which `tidyr` comes handy.

How to do it...

1. Create a data frame with your data:

    ```
    messy_gdp <- import("world_gdp_data.csv")
    ```

2. Apply the `gather()` function to your data frame:

    ```
    tidy_gdp   <- gather(messy_gdp,"year","gdp",5:61)
    ```

3. Visualize the result with the RStudio viewer:

    ```
    View(tidy_gdp)
    ```

How it works...

In step 1, we create a data frame with our data. This step leverages the `rio` package, which is treated in the *Loading your data into R with rio packages* recipe in *Chapter 1, Acquiring Data for Your Project*. Refer to it for further explanations.

In step 2, we apply the `gather()` function to our data frame. The `gather()` functions is one of the four functions available within the `tidyr` package:

*   `gather()`
*   `spread()`
*   `unite()`
*   `separate()`

This function basically retrieves values spread within the messy dataset and creates a new data frame where those values are exposed, following a `key` attribute.

More formally, here we take a dataset exposed in a wide form and transform it into a long form dataset.

In our example, values are annual GDP and keys are years.

The `gather()` function requires you to specify the following arguments:

*   Data
*   Name to assign to the key column
*   Name to assign to the value column
*   Columns in which to find values
*   All other columns will be left unchanged and their values will be repeated as needed

In step 3, we visualize the result with the RStudio viewer. One of the most powerful RStudio tools is the data viewer, which lets you get a spreadsheet-like view of your data frames. With RStudio 0.99 Version, this tool got even more powerful, removing the previous 1000-row limit and adding the ability to filter and order your data.

When using this viewer, you should be aware that all filtering and ordering activities will not affect the original data frame object you are visualizing.

There's more...

As seen earlier, in addition to `gather()`, paragraph, the `tidyr` package supplies the following three functions for data preparation:

The `spread()` function is used when variables are stored in a column, as is the case in the following dataset, named:

- second_messy_world_gdp:

  ```
  country, data ,value
  italy, year, 2012
  italy,gdp, 20000
  russia,year,2012
  russia,gdp,1100000
  ```

- Running `spread(messy_world_gdp, data,value)` will result in the following tidy dataset:

  - tidy_world_gdp:

    ```
    country, year, gdp
    italy,2012,20000
    russia,2012,1100000
    ```

The `separate()` function is used when two or more variables are stored in a single column joined side by side:

- third_messy_world_gdp:

  ```
  country, year_gdp
  italy,2012_20000
  russia,2012_1100000
  ```

In this case, running `separate(messy_world_gdp,year_gdp,c("year","gdp"),sep ="_")` will result in the following tidy data frame:

- country, year, gdp

  ```
  italy,2012,20000
  russia,2012,1100000
  ```

The `unite()` function can be considered the opposite of `separate()` and can be used when a single variable is spread among different columns. Here is an example:

▸ `fourth_messy_world_gdp`:

```
year, month,day, value
2012,12,31,120003
2012,05,12,4533203
```

In this case, we can join the first free columns, creating a date variable simply by running `unite(fourth_messy_world_gdp,col = "record_date",c(year,month,day,),` `sep = "_")`, which will result in the following tidy data frame:

```
record_date, value
2012_12_31,120003
2012_05_12,4533203
```

Please note that both the `separate()` and `unite()` functions require us to specify a `sep` parameter, indicating in the first case the character to look for in order to perform the column separation, and in the second case the argument that will be used as a joining character between the column values.

More about tidy data and its use can be found in the paper *Tidy data*, written by Hadley Wickham, the main author of the package. The paper is freely available at `http://www.jstatsoft.org/article/view/v059i10`.

Detecting and removing missing values

Missing values are values that should have been recorded but, for some reason, weren't actually recorded. Those values are different, from values without meaning, represented in R with **NaN** (**not a number**).

Most of us understood missing values due to circumstances such as the following one:

```
> x <- c(1,2,3,NA,4)

> mean(x)

[1] NA
```

"Oh come on, I know you can do it. Just ignore that useless NA" was probably your reaction, or at least it was mine.

Fortunately, R comes packed with good functions for missing value detection and handling.

In this recipe and the following one, we will see two opposite approaches to missing value handling:

- Removing missing values
- Simulating missing values by interpolation

I have to warn you that removing missing values can be considered right in a really small number of cases, since it compromises the integrity of your data sources and can greatly reduce the reliability of your results.

Nevertheless, if you are strongly willing to do this, I will show you how to do it in a really effective way, using the `md.pattern()` and `complete.cases()` functions from the mice package by Stef van Buuren.

Getting ready

Before applying this recipe, you will need to install and load the mice package:

```
install.packages("mice")
library(mice)
```

How to do it...

1. Find where the missing values are located:

   md.pattern(tidy_gdp)

   This will result in an output similar to the following screenshot:

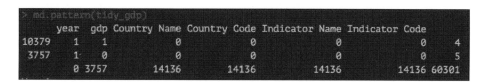

   It shows us that in `10379` cases, `Country Name`, `Country Code`, `Indicator Name`, and `Indicator Code` are missing, and in `3757` cases, only the year is present and the rest is missing.

2. Remove rows where data for a given column are missing:

   tidy_gdp_naomit <- subset(tidy_gdp,

   tidy_gdp$gdp!=complete.cases(tidy_gdp$gdp))

   The `tidy_gdp_naomit` command will now contain only observations where GDP was actually recorded.

3. Check the result:

```
md.pattern(tidy_gdp_naomit)
```

It should now result in a matrix where no missing value cases are shown for the gdp column:

```
> md.pattern(tidy_gdp_naomit)
     year gdp Country Name Country Code Indicator Name Indicator Code
[1,]    1   1            0            0              0              0     4
[2,]    0   0        10379        10379          10379          10379 41516
```

How it works...

In step 1, we find where missing values are located. The `md.pattern()` function from the `mice` package is a really useful function. It gives you a clear view of where missing values are located, helping you in decisions regarding exclusions or substitution. You can refer to the next recipe for missing value substitution.

In step 2, we remove rows where data for a given column is missing. The `Complete.cases()` function lists all the data in a vector not equal to NA. By posing `tidy_gdp$gdp!=complete.cases(tidy_gdp$gdp)`, we are just filtering for all the data available.

In step 3, we check the result using the `md.pattern()` function once again so that we can easily check for the persistence of NA values after our detection and removal procedures.

There's more...

Another way to deal with missing values is simply ignoring them in our computations. This is a built-in option for a really large number of R functions. It is usually expressed with the `na.rm` argument. A useful piece of advice to keep in mind is that ignoring NA values is not always a solution without consequences.

Take, for instance, the average computation on the following records vector:

```
records <- c(NA,4,3,6,NA)
```

Let's ignore NA values by posing the `na.rm` argument as `true`:

```
mean_na_ignoring <- mean(records, na.rm = TRUE)
```

We will obtain:

```
[1] 4.333333
```

This is a really different number from the one we will obtain when considering missing values as records with 0 value:

```
records ← x[is.na(x)] <- 0
> mean(records)
[1] 2.6
```

This simple example shows you why missing values need to be handled carefully.

Substituting missing values using the mice package

Finding and removing missing values in your dataset is not always a viable alternative, for either operative or methodological reasons. It is often preferable to simulate possible values for missing data and integrate those values within the observed data.

This recipe is based on the `mice` package by Stef van Buuren. It provides an efficient algorithm for missing value substitution based on the multiple imputation technique.

Multiple imputation technique

The multiple imputation technique is a statistical solution to the problem of missing values.

The main idea behind this technique is to draw possible alternative values for each missing value and then, after a proper analysis of simulated values, populating the original dataset with synthetic data.

Getting ready

This recipe requires that you install and load the mice package:

```
install.packages("mice")
library(mice)
```

For illustrative purposes, we will use the `tidy_gdp` data frame created in the *Preparing your data for analysis with* the *tidyr package* recipe. This dataset is provided with the RStudio project for this book. You can download it by authenticating your account at `http://packtpub.com`.

In order to make missing values appear, we will have to transform the value column type from characters to numbers:

```
tidy_gdp$gdp <- as.numeric(tidy_gdp$gdp)
```

As shown in the previous recipe, you can now look for missing value patterns by leveraging the `md.pattern()` function:

```
md.pattern(tidy_gdp$gdp)
```

	year	gdp	Country Name	Country Code	Indicator Name	Indicator Code
103794	1	1	0	0	0	0
37575	1	0	0	0	0	0
	0	3757	14136	14136	14136	14136
60301						

How to do it...

1. Generate the data to substitute missing values using the `mice()` function:

   ```
   simulation   <- mice(tidy_gdp, method = "pmm")
   ```

   The console will then print the following output:

   ```
   iter imp variable
    1    1  gdp
    1    2  gdp
    1    3  gdp
    1    4  gdp
    1    5  gdp
    2    1  gdp
    2    2  gdp
    2    3  gdp
    2    4  gdp
    2    5  gdp
    3    1  gdp
    3    2  gdp
    3    3  gdp
    3    4  gdp
    3    5  gdp
    4    1  gdp
    4    2  gdp
    4    3  gdp
    4    4  gdp
   ```

```
4    5   gdp
5    1   gdp
5    2   gdp
5    3   gdp
5    4   gdp
5    5   gdp
```

2. Populate the original data with generated data:

```
tidy_gdp_complete ← complete(simulation, action =1)
```

3. Check the reasonableness of the generated values:

```
densityplot(simulation)
```

This function will show a plot representing simulated data in red and recorded data in blue. If the two `density()` functions differ too much, this would mean that the resulting dataset should be considered unreliable:

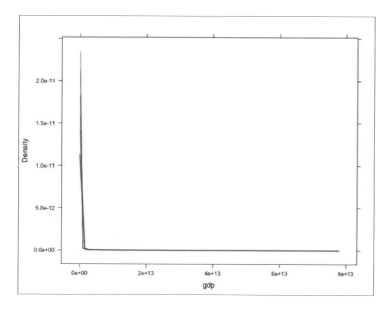

4. Iterate the procedure until you get satisfactory results.

If the check results in simulated data that is not reasonable, you should consider changing the statistical method used to generate data. You may also abandon the idea of using synthetic data, particularly if the missing value/recorded value ratio is really high.

How it works...

In step 1, we generate data to substitute missing values using the `mice()` function. This step leverages the `mice()` function to produce multiple possible values to be used as substitutes for missing values within the `tidy_gdp` data frame.

The number of possible values to be produced for each missing value is determined by the `m` parameter, set by default to `5`. This is usually a sufficient number of iterations. However, especially with unsuccessful results, you could consider incrementing the number of simulations.

In step 2, we populate the original data with generated data. This step is easily performed using the `complete()` function, which lets you choose between the number of m values generated for any missing value. Then, substitute it for the missing one. This choice is made by specifying the `action` parameter.

In step 3, we check for the reasonableness of the generated values. Using the `densityplot()` function from the `lattice` package (it should be preinstalled with every distribution of R), we can easily assess whether simulated values are reasonable compared to observed values.

In step 4, we iterate until we get satisfactory results. In the case of negative feedback from the density plot, you should consider changing the statistical method used to generate the missing values, as showed in the *There's more...* section.

There's more...

Different simulation methods are available within the `mice()` function. These methods can be selected using the `method` argument:

- `pmm` (predictive mean matching)
- `logreg` (logistic regression imputation)
- `polyreg` (polytomous regression imputation)
- `polr` (proportional odds model)

If no value is provided, the `mice()` function will automatically select a method, depending on the data type, by following those rules:

- Numeric data → predictive mean matching
- Binary data/factor with two levels → logistic regression imputation
- Unordered categorical data with two or more levels → polytomous regression imputation
- Ordered categorical data with two or more levels → proportional odds model

You can find more methods in the `mice()` function documentation by running the following command:

```
?mice()
```

If you are dealing with missing values, you will find another great ally in the VIM package. This package also provides tools for the visualization of missing and/or imputed values.

You can find out more on this package in the official reference manual at `https://cran.r-project.org/web/packages/VIM/VIM.pdf`.

Detecting and removing outliers

Outliers are usually dangerous values for data science activities, since they produce heavy distortions within models and algorithms.

Their detection and exclusion is, therefore, a really crucial task.

This recipe will show you how to easily perform this task.

We will compute the I and IV quartiles of a given population and detect values that far from these fixed limits.

You should note that this recipe is feasible only for univariate quantitative population, while different kind of data will require you to use other outlier-detection methods.

How to do it...

1. Compute the quantiles using the `quantile()` function:

   ```
   quantiles <- quantile(tidy_gdp_complete$gdp, probs = c(.25, .75))
   ```

2. Compute the range value using the `IQR()` function:

   ```
   range <- 1.5 * IQR(tidy_gdp_complete$gdp)
   ```

3. Subset the original data by excluding the outliers:

   ```
   normal_gdp <- subset(tidy_gdp_complete,
   tidy_gdp_complete$gdp > (quantiles[1] - range) & tidy_gdp_complete$gdp < (quantiles[2] + range))
   ```

How it works...

In step 1, we compute quantiles using the `quantile()` function. This implementation of outlier detection and removal is based on the most classical outlier detection technique. It requires you to exclude all values below the second quartile and above the third quartile, both incremented of a measure equal to 1.5 times the interquartile range. First, you need to define the second and third quartiles using the `quantile()` function, passing at least the following arguments:

- The data for which you want to compute quartiles. Be aware that you need to pass the column and not the entire dataset.

- The quartile you want to compute as a vector. Since the function is built in order to let you retrieve any of the 100 quantiles computable for a population, you have to express the desired quartile as a number between `0` and `1`.

In step 2, we compute the range value using the `IQR()` function. Using the `IQR()` function, you can easily obtain the interquartile range for a given numeric vector. No additional parameter is needed.

In step 3, we subset the original data, excluding outliers. The final step requires you to apply the `subset()` function and exclude all values lying outside the range delimited from the second quartile—1.5*interquartile range and the third quartile + 1.5*interquartile range.

Performing data filtering activities

This is a bit of a recap recipe. In the workflow proposed here, we will sum up the tricks and knowledge gained throughout the book in order to perform a data-filtering activity.

Data filtering includes all the activities performed on a dataset to make it ready for further analysis.

Isn't it the same as data cleansing?

Well, in a sense... yes. However, not exactly the same, since data filtering usually refers to some specific techniques and not to others, while data cleansing can be considered a more comprehensive concept.

That said, here we will make tests for our data frame, performing subsequent filtering activities and reporting about these activities. The following diagram shows the flow:

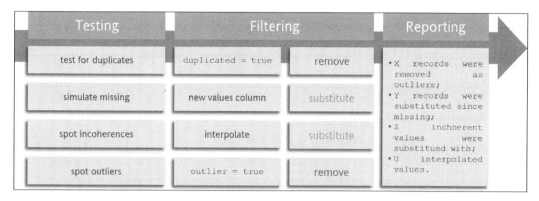

Testing	Filtering		Reporting
test for duplicates	duplicated = true	remove	• X records were removed as outliers;
simulate missing	new values column	substitute	• Y records were substituted since missing;
spot incoherences	interpolate	substitute	• Z inchoerent values were substitued with;
spot outliers	outlier = true	remove	• U interpolated values.

As you can see in the diagram, we will:

- ▸ Look for duplicated values and remove them
- ▸ Substitute by simulation missing values, as explained in the preceding recipe
- ▸ Interpolate incoherent values, which are multiple values for a given attribute
- ▸ Remove outliers, as seen in the preceding recipe

At the end of all these filtering activities, we will make our code produce a detailed report on the activities performed and results obtained.

The main value added here is to show how these activities can be performed as a unique workflow. This is actually quite common in real-life data analysis projects, where some tasks are preliminarily performed before we go on to the main activities.

To stress the point of the flow, I also suggest that you refer to the *There's more...* section to learn how to transform this flow within a custom function in order to let you apply it quickly every time you need it.

Getting ready

Before actually working on our data frame, we will create it here.

As mentioned earlier, we want to find outliers, incoherences, missing values, and duplicates. So, let's create a really bad data frame containing all these problems.

First, we will create a good dataset with data related to payments received from a customer:

```
dataset <- data.frame(
  key       = seq (1:251),
  date      = seq(as.Date("2012/5/12"), as.Date("2013/1/17"), by
  = "day"),
```

```
        attributes = c(rep("cash",times = 110),rep("transfer", times =
        141)),
        value      = rnorm(251, mean = 100)
    )
```

Our data frame will now have:

- A key column from 1 to 251.
- A date column with dates from May 12, 2012 to January 17, 2013.
- An attribute showing the kind of payment received, either cash or bank transfer.
- A value column, with values taken from a normal distribution with mean 100 (I used normal distribution just because it is cool, but data distribution is absolutely irrelevant here). Now that we have got a healthy data frame, it is time to make it sick.

Let's start mixing payment types, just to be more realistic:

```
for (i in 1:120) {
    dataset[round(runif(1, 1,251)),3] <- dataset[round(runif(1,
    1,251)),3]
}
```

Here, we will take a value from a randomly selected cell of the `attributes` column and put it into another randomly selected cell within the `attributes` column. We will do this 120 times with a `for` loop.

We will use `runif()` to select a first random number to use as the row index (we ask for a number between 1 and 251, the number of total rows). The value corresponding to the randomly selected row within the `attributes` column is then assigned to another randomly selected row within the `attributes` column.

Keep this process in mind, since we will use it again within a few lines.

Now, it is time to duplicate some values:

```
for (i in 1:20) {
    dataset[round(runif(1, 1,251)),] <- dataset[round(runif(1,
    1,251)),]
}
```

We randomly copied (select) a row and pasted it into another row, overwriting the old one.

Time to make some outliers:

```
for (i in 1:3) {
    index <- round(runif(1, 1,251))
    dataset[index,4] <- dataset[index,4]*1.3
}
```

What are outliers? Values outside the crowd. So, we took a member of the crowd and multiplied it 1.3 times. Is that arbitrary? Yes it is, but from the *Detecting and removing outliers* recipe, you should know that even outlier detection is in some way arbitrary.

To create incoherences, which we will remove later, we just have to copy a `date` attribute and paste it randomly. This will produce more than one value for the same date:

```
for (i in 1:15) {
  dataset[round(runif(1, 1,251)),2] <- dataset[round(runif(1,
  1,251)),2]
}
```

Creating missing values is the simplest task. You just need to take some random rows and set the `value` attribute for that row to `NA`:

```
for (i in 1:10) {
  dataset[round(runif(1, 1,251)),4] <- NA
}
```

It is now time to install and load the required packages:

```
install.packages("mice","dplyr")
library(mice)
library(dplyr)
```

How to do it...

1. Store the number of rows within the original dataset:

   ```
   n_of_initial_records <- nrow(dataset)
   ```

2. Compute the number of duplicates and store it:

   ```
   n_duplicates <- sum(duplicated(dataset))
   ```

3. Detect duplicated rows and delete them:

   ```
   dataset <- distinct(dataset)
   ```

4. Store the number of NAs:

   ```
   n_na <- nrow(subset(dataset,is.na(dataset$value)))
   ```

5. Simulate possible values for missing values and substitute them:

   ```
   simulation_data   <- mice(dataset[,-2], method = "pmm")
   simulated_data    <- complete(simulation_data)
   dataset$simulated <- simulated_data$value
   ```

6. Sort the dataset by date (or alternative key to spot incoherences):

   ```
   dataset <- dataset[order(dataset$date),]
   ```

7. Count the number of values for each date and store repeated dates with their frequency in the data frame:

```
dates_frequency <- table(dataset$date)
dates_count <-    data.frame(dates_frequency)
colnames(dates_count) <- c("date","frequency")
dates_repeated_count <-
subset(dates_count,dates_count$frequency > 1)
```

8. Create a vector with repeated dates:

```
dates_repeated_list <-
as.Date(as.character(dates_repeated_count$date))
```

9. Define the number of interpolated data (where the number of repeated dates is equal to the number of interpolated values):

```
n_of_interpolated <- nrow(dates_repeated_count)
```

10. Define the number of records removed because of incoherences:

```
n_of_removed_for_interpolation <-
sum(dates_repeated_count$frequency)
```

11. Interpolate values by computing the average of the previous and subsequent values:

```
for (i in 1:length(dates_repeated_list)) {
  i = 1
  date_match_index <-
  match(dates_repeated_list[i],dataset$date)
  number_of_repeat    <- dates_repeated_count[i,2]
  # find value for 1 day before and one day after, handling
  hypotesis of the first or the last value
  # in dataset being incoherent
  if(date_match_index == 1 | date_match_index ==
  nrow(dataset)) {
    value_before = mean(dataset$simulated)
    value_after = mean(dataset$simulated)

  }
  else {
    value_before <- dataset$value[date_match_index-1]
    value_after <-
  dataset$value[date_match_index+number_of_repeat+1]
  }
  }
  # compute average
  interpolated_value   <- mean(c(value_after,value_before))
  # create a a new row with same date and average value
```

```
interpolated_record <-
data.frame(dataset[date_match_index,1:4],"simulated"
=interpolated_value)
# add interpolated record to general dataset
dataset <- rbind(dataset,interpolated_record)
# remove incoherencies
dataset <- dataset[-
(date_match_index:date_match_index+number_of_repeat),]
}
```

12. Spot and remove outliers by storing the number of removed rows:

```
dataset_quantiles <- quantile(dataset$simulated, probs =
c(0.25,0.75))
range <- 1.5 * IQR(dataset$simulated)
n_outliers <- nrow(subset(dataset, dataset$simulated <
(dataset_quantiles[1] - range) | dataset$simulated >
(dataset_quantiles[2] + range)) )
dataset <- subset(dataset, dataset$simulated >=
(dataset_quantiles[1] - range) & dataset$simulated <=
(dataset_quantiles[2] + range))
```

13. Build a filtering activity report:

```
filtering_report <- paste0("FILTERING ACTIVITIES REPORT:
\n\n - ", n_outliers, " records were removed as outliers;\n
- ", n_na," records were substituted since missing;\n - ",
n_of_removed_for_interpolation," inchoerent values were
substitued with;\n - ", n_of_interpolated, " interpolated
values.\n\n"," ", n_of_initial_records, " original
records\n", " (-) ",
n_outliers+n_of_removed_for_interpolation," removed\n", "
(+) ", n_of_interpolated, " added\n", " = ", nrow(dataset),
" total records for filtered dataset")
```

14. Visualize your report:

```
message (filtering_report)
```

How it works...

In step 1, we store the number of rows within the original dataset. This step is required to provide a detailed report about the activities performed at the end of the process. We count the number of rows in the original dataset by running `nrow()` on the dataset.

In step 2, we compute the number of duplicates and store it. How would you compute the number of duplicated rows?

We use the `duplicated()` function from base R. Running this function on the dataset results in a vector with the value `True` for every duplicated record and `False` for unique values.

We then sum up this vector, obtaining the number of duplicated rows.

We store the result of this basic computation in a variable to be employed later, in the reporting phase.

In step 3, we detect duplicated rows and delete them. In this step, we apply the `distinct()` function from the `dplyr` package. This function removes duplicated values within a data frame, leaving only unique records.

You may find it interesting to know that this function offers the ability to look not only for entirely duplicated rows, but also for duplicated values. This can be done by specifying the attribute against which you want to look for duplicates.

Let's have a look at this basic example to understand how:

```
data <- data.frame("alfa"= c("a","b","b", "b"), "beta" =
c(1,2,4,4))
```

As you can see, this data frame contains three duplicated values on column `alfa` and two completely duplicated values, the last two.

Let' try to remove the last two rows by running `distinct()` on the whole dataset:

This will result in the following dataset:

	alfa	beta
1	a	1
2	b	2
3	b	4

But what if we run distinct, specifying we want to look for duplicates only within the `alfa` column?

```
distinct(data,alfa)
```

This will result in the following print:

	alfa	beta
1	a	1
2	b	2

Here we are. We filtered the dataset only for rows where the `alfa` attribute is duplicated.

In step 4, we store the number of NAs. We skip to missing value handling. First, we store the number of missing values, counting the number of rows in a dataset resulted from a subset of the original one.

We filtered the `dataset` object in order to keep only missing values, using the `is.na()` function of base R. The number of rows in this dataset will be exactly the number of missing values within the original dataset.

In step 5, we simulate possible values for missing values and substitute them. This step leverages missing value handling techniques learned in the *Substituting missing values using the mice package* recipe introduced previously. You can find more details on its rationales and results in that recipe.

All we have to specify here is that after running this piece of code, we will have a new column within our dataset, a new column with no missing values. This column will be used as the value column.

In step 6, we sort the dataset by date (or alternative key to spot incoherences). This step starts the treatment of incoherences. It is actually a soft start, since we just order by date. Nevertheless, let me explain this briefly.

What we want to find out now is the presence of more records for a given attribute. In our example, we are assuming that the attribute is the day. We are therefore stating that if more than one payment was recorded for a unique day, an error must have occurred within the recording process, and we are going to treat these records as incoherent.

You can see that the date is only an example, since the key could be any kind of attribute, or even more than one attribute.

For instance, we could impose a constraint of this type:

- If more than one payment was recorded for a customer (first key) within a single day (second key), something must have occurred.

What is the bottom line here? Sort by your relevant attribute, not necessarily by the date.

In step 7, we count the number of values for each date and store in a data frame repeated dates, with their frequencies.

It is now time to find incoherent records. First, we will find them by counting how many times each date is recorded within the dataset.

This can be done by leveraging the `table()` function from base R. This function computes a frequency table for a given attribute within a dataset.

The resulting `dates_frequency` object will have the following shape:

```
Var1           Freq

2012-05-12     1

2012-05-13     1

2012-05-12     2
```

Given the explanation in the previous step, which of these lines underline incoherences? Those where `Freq` is greater than 1, since these cases show that more than one value was recorded for the same date.

That is why we create `dates_repeated_count`, a data frame containing only dates with a frequency greater than 1.

In step 8, we create a vector with repeated dates. This is quite a tricky step. To understand it, we need to think about the class of the `date` column in the date `repeated_count`.

Here is how we can do it.

We can run the `str()` function on it to understand which class is assigned to the date column:

```
> str(dates_repeated_count)
'data.frame': 13 obs. of  2 variables:
$ date      : Factor w/ 219 levels "2012-05-12","2012-05-13",..: 10 22 29
107 119 126 128 145 148 153 ...
 $ frequency: int  2 2 2 2 2 2 2 2 2 2 …
```

As you see, date is a `Factor` with 219 values, one for each unique date. Generally speaking, the `Factor` class is a really convenient class to handle categorical variables. In our case, we will need to transform it into a `Date` class.

Why? Because the column we will compare it with was defined as a `Date` column!

Casting is done using these two steps:

- First, we change the format from factor to character using the `as.character()` function
- Then, we transform the character function in the data using the `as.date()` function

At the end of the process, we will have a new vector of class `Date` that stores only dates for which some incoherence was underlined.

In step 9, we define the number of interpolated data (where the number of repeated dates = the number of interpolated values). This step is within the family of *accounting* steps already performed. We just compute and store the number of interpolated values. How do we compute them? We just have to compute the number of repeated dates, since we will define an interpolated value for each incoherence.

This is exactly what we do when we count the number of rows within the `dates_repeated_count`.

In step 10, we define the number of records removed because of incoherences. Here, we want to understand and memorize how many records will be removed because they come, we assume, from errors within the recording process.

This number will equal the sum of the `Freq` column within the dataset that stores all repeated dates. Why?

Because the number of times a duplicated date is recorded within the original dataset is equal to the number of incoherent records for that date. Therefore, the sum of the number of times all duplicated dates are recorded within the original dataset will equal the total number of incoherences and therefore equal the number of records removed because they were incoherent.

It's a bit of a devious trip I know, but I am sure you have followed me.

In step 11, we interpolate values by computing the average of the previous and subsequent values. This is the actual core part of our treatment of incoherences.

In this step, we looped through all the dates where incoherences were found, which are stored within the previously defined `dates_repeated_list`. We defined an interpolated value for each of these dates.

Our interpolation approach is as follows:

- We look for the record before the duplicated date and store it within the `value_before` object
- We look for the record after the duplicated date and store it within the `value_after` object
- We compute the mean of these two values

Here is a graphical explanation of this approach:

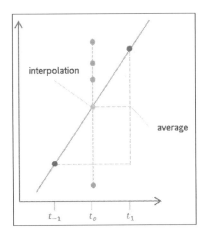

As you can see, we do not consider incoherent values and actually remove them from the dataset. Be aware that two special cases are handled in a quite different way. If incoherences are within the first or the last date, we simply interpolate using the mean of the overall value vector.

In step 12, we spot and remove outliers by storing the number of removed rows. Removing outliers was a task we performed in the *Detecting and removing outliers* recipe. Refer to this recipe to understand how we do this.

We need to ensure that the number of outliers removed is stored within the n_outliers variable.

In step 13, we build a filtering activity report. I have to admit this is one of my favorite parts. We sum up all the stored numbers by composing a detailed report on the activities performed and their results.

To accomplish this task, we created a vector by pasting together strings and numbers stored within the entire analysis.

I would like to highlight the use of the \n token to start a new paragraph.

In step 14, we visualize the report. Running the (filtering_report) message will make your report appear on your console. As you can see, on reading the report, we can understand the impact of each activity performed and reconcile the original number of rows with the final one. This is a really useful feature, particularly when sharing the results of your activities with colleagues or external validators.

3
Basic Visualization Techniques

In this chapter, we will cover the following recipes:

- ▸ Looking at your data using the `plot()` function
- ▸ Using `pairs.panel()` to look at (visualize) correlations between variables
- ▸ Adding text to a `ggplot2` plot at a custom location
- ▸ Changing axes appearance to `ggplot2` plot
- ▸ Producing a matrix of graphs with `ggplot2`
- ▸ Drawing a route on a map with `ggmap`
- ▸ Making use of the `igraph` package to draw a network
- ▸ Showing communities in a network with the `linkcomm` package

Introduction

You now have your data in R (as discussed in *Chapter 1, Acquiring Data for Your Project*) and you gained a good understanding of its structure (in *Chapter 2, Preparing for Analysis – Data Cleansing and Manipulation*), but do you have an idea of its, let's say, appearance?

Do you know how data is related to itself? Do any correlations exist?

If you want to model your phenomenon with accuracy and effectiveness, you have to know the answers to these questions. This is where basic data visualization comes in handy. This includes plotting your variables against one another, looking for correlations, understanding relations (or absence of relations) without losing yourself in hundreds of lines of code.

In this chapter, we will do all of this mainly using base R and `ggplot2`, which is the data visualization package that lets you produce plots by applying the grammar of graphics and has become a standard of R dataviz.

Besides basic data visualizations recipes, some goodies are also provided in this chapter, such as the recipe that lets you place text at a custom location on your `ggplot` or the one about axis manipulation with `ggplot2`.

These recipes are provided here to let you get sufficient control over your plots and make them a sound basis for the next data analysis activities.

Looking at your data using the plot() function

The `plot()` function is one of most powerful functions in base R. The main point of using the `plot()` function is that it will always try to print out a representation of your data. It basically tries to figure out which kind of representation is the best, based on the data type. This will let you easily and quickly get a first view of the data you are working with.

Behind the scenes, the power of the `plot()` function comes from being packed with a number of methods developed for specific types of object.

So, when an object is passed as an argument to `plot()`, it looks for the most appropriate method within the ones available and uses it to represent data stored within the object.

It is even possible to further expand the `plot()` function, as is regularly done in various packages, adding new methods for specific types of object by running `setMethod()` on it. This is out of the scope of this recipe, but you can find a good explanation in the R language documentation at `https://stat.ethz.ch/R-manual/R-devel/library/methods/html/setMethod.html`.

Getting ready

Just like all other recipes in this chapter, we will use the *iris* dataset as a sample dataset. You will find this dataset in every installation of the R environment.

The iris dataset is one of most used datasets in R tutorials and learning sessions, and is derived from a 1936 paper *The use of multiple measurements in taxonomic problems*, by Ronald Fisher.

50 samples of 3 species of the iris flower were observed:

- ▶ Iris setosa
- ▶ Iris virginica
- ▶ Iris versicolor

For each sample, four features were recorded:

- ▸ Length of the sepals
- ▸ Width of the sepals
- ▸ Length of the petals
- ▸ Width of the petals

To get an idea of this dataset, you can take a look at its structure by running the following code:

```
str(iris)
```

Well, to be honest, if you arrived here after walking through *Chapter 2, Preparing for Analysis – Data Cleansing and Manipulation*, understanding the structure of your data shouldn't be a problem for you. Nevertheless, you can always skip back to that chapter, specifically to the *Getting a sense of your data structure with R* recipe.

How to do it...

1. Visualize your data by applying the `plot()` function:

   ```
   plot(iris)
   ```

   This will result into the following plot:

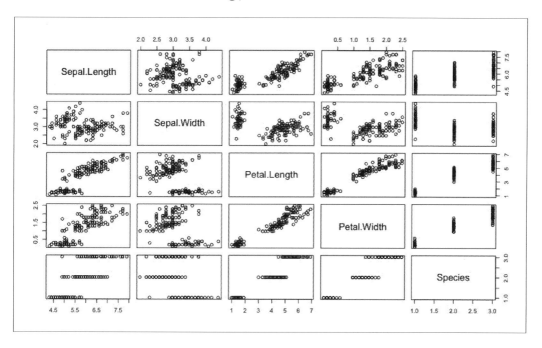

The preceding plot shows all variables against one other, for instance, the second rectangle in the first row from the top shows **Sepal.Length** against **Sepal.Width** while the third shows **Sepal.Length** against **Petal.Length**.

As you may have probably noted, the plot makes it easier to spot the presence, or absence, of any relationship between variables.

1. Select a particular attribute to visualize.

    Among the attributes recorded for each observation, you can easily select a specific attribute by running the following code:

    ```
    plot(iris$Sepal.Width)
    ```

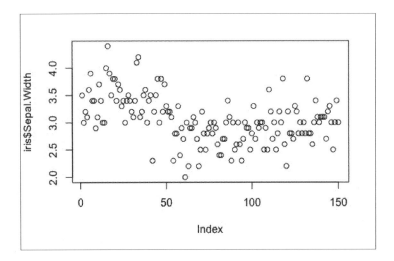

    The resulting plot shows on the *x* axis the row index of a given observation, which, as per the data frame dimensions, ranges from 0 to 150. On the *y* axis, you will find the value of the particular attribute *y*.

    Select which is, in our example, **Sepa.Width** column.

2. Change the plot type.

   You can change the type of plot produced by the `plot ()` function by changing the value of the `type` argument.

   Let's try with the value 0, which stands for points and lines overplotted:

   ```
   plot(iris$Sepal.Width,type = "h")
   ```

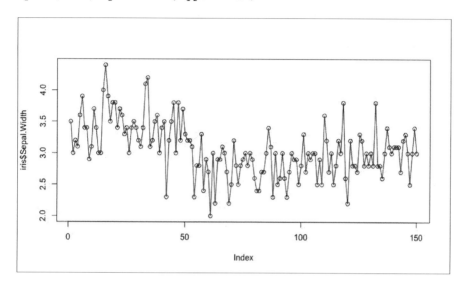

3. Focus on another variable or a couple of variables.

   You can now focus on different variables or even plot two plots against each other using the following script:

   ```
   plot(x = iris$petal.length, y = iris$petal.width)
   ```

How it works...

As discussed in the introduction to this recipe, the plot function basically looks at the data type of plotting object and subsequently chooses an appropriate way to display it.

For instance in step 1, if plotting a simple vector, the `plot()` function will plot it against the vector indexes:

```
x <- c(1,2,3)
plot(x)
```

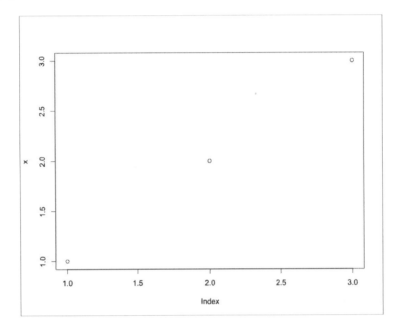

If we plot the same vector together with another vector, the two of them stored in a dataframe will instead result in a scatter plot with the two vectors on the axes:

```
x <- c(1,2,3)
y <- c(4,6,8)
data <- data.frame(x,y)
plot(data)
```

Consequently, passing a data frame composed of different *n* attributes and therefore *n* columns to the `plot()` function will result in a matrix of *n x n* columns where each attribute is plotted against the other, as seen in the recipe.

By now, you know what step 2 is all about. Plotting iris$sepal.length alone results in a plot where *x* axis is represented by row indexes of the iris dataset the, while the sepal.length values are represented on the *y* axis.

Besides great flexibility on the input side, in step 3, the `plot()` function is characterized by a good number of possible choices for the output.

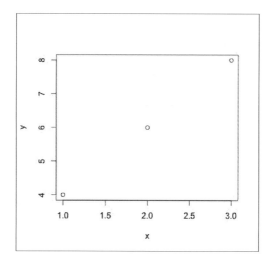

In particular, changing the value of the `type` argument makes it possible to change the type of data visualization that the plot will produce.

You can choose from among the following possibilities:

▸ **p** for **p**oints (when plotting two variables this will result in a scatterplot)

▸ **l** for **l**ines

▸ **b** for **b**oth

▸ **c** for the lines part alone of **b**

▸ **o** for both **o**verplotted

▸ **h** for **h**istogram-like (or high-density) vertical lines

▸ **s** for stair **s**teps

▸ **S** for other **s**teps-refer to details provided later

▸ **n** for **n**o plotting

All these types are available for numerical variables, while more attention has to be paid to categorical attributes.

► Step 4 explains that plotting a categorical variable using the `plot()` function by specifying a `type` argument will always result in a histogram representing the number of occurrences of each possible value assumed by the attribute:

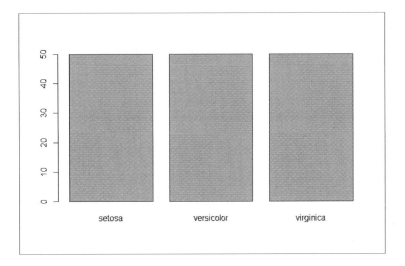

► Be aware that while plotting two numerical variables will result in a scatter plot, plotting a categorical variable against a numerical one will result in a box plot, depicting the distribution of a given numerical variable within each subgroup defined from the categorical attribute:

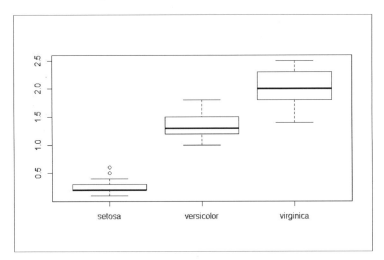

Using pairs.panel() to look at (visualize) correlations between variables

Within the R ecosystem, there are different packages offering ways to represent correlations between variables in a dataset.

In a way, the powerful `plot()` function, as seen in the previous recipe, can also be useful for correlation spotting, particularly when plotting all variables against one another (refer to the previous recipe for more details).

Nevertheless, among different alternatives, the one I think may give you a quicker and deeper understanding of the relationship between your data is the `pairs.panels()` function provided by the `psych` package by William Revelle.

Getting ready

In order to use the `pairs.panels()` function, we first need to install and load the `psych` package:

```
install.packages("psych")
library(psych)
```

To test the `pairs.panels()` functionality, we will use the Iris dataset.

The Iris dataset is one of most used datasets in R tutorials and learning sessions, and it is derived from a 1936 paper by Ronald Fisher, named The use of multiple measurements in taxonomic problems.

Data was observed on 50 samples of three species of the iris flower:

- Iris setosa
- Iris virginica
- Iris versicolor

On each sample for features were recorded:

- length of the sepals
- width of the sepals
- length of the petals
- width of the petals

In the following example, we will look for correlations between these variables.

How to do it...

1. Visualize your dataset using `pairs.panels()`:

```
pairs.panels(iris, hist.col = "white", ellipses = FALSE)
```

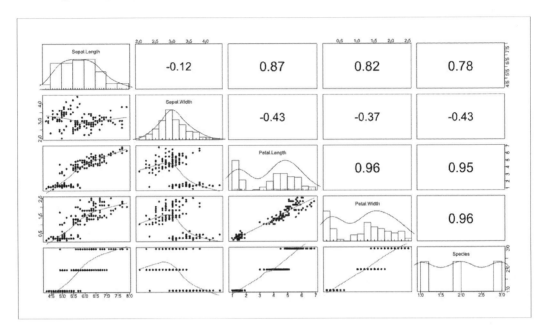

How it works...

The `pairs.panels()` function produces quite a comprehensive plot, showing in one picture the following things:

▶ The correlation coefficient between all variables (numbers on the upper-right side of the plot) lets you understand whether a linear correlation is present between your variables

▶ The frequency distribution (the histograms on the diagonal) lets you quickly visualize the typical values of your data and the general distribution shapes of your variables

▶ The scatterplot among variables in pairs lets you visually find non-linear correlations

Some aesthetic parameters are set within the function call; these involve colors for the histograms bars and the plotting of correlation ellipses. You can refer to the *There's more...* section in this recipe for more details on these arguments.

There's more...

The `pairs.panels()` function allows you to customize the output; some customizations are purely pertaining to aesthetics and others are related to the computations that happen behind the panel visualization.

Part of the first group is the `hist.col` argument, which will set the color of the distribution plots produced by the function.

It is also possible to change methods for correlation computation, leveraging the method argument.

The following methods are available:

▶ Pearson

▶ Spearman

▶ Kendall

We can also specify if correlation ellipses, also named confidence or error ellipses, should be added to our plot through, as you may have probably guessed, the `ellipses` argument.

Adding text to a ggplot2 plot at a custom location

When displaying the results of your analysis, even if at exploratory stages, it is crucial to have the ability to customize your data visualization.

One thing I always find particularly useful is using the text annotations on your plot to highlight the findings in the most effective way.

In `ggplot2`, you can do this using the `geom_text()` function, moving your string around the plot to adjust the `position` argument. So, you will have to try and try again until you find the correct position for your handful of words. But, what if you could just select a location for your text by just clicking on it with your cursor?

That is exactly what this recipe is for; you will be able to add a custom text on your plot and place it at the defined location with a simple click on the plot itself.

Getting ready

We first need to install and load the `ggplot2` and `ggmap` packages:

```
install.packages(c("ggplot2","ggmap"))
library(ggplot2)
library(ggmap)
```

How to do it...

1. Build the `ggplot2` plot and print it.

   Define a basic `ggplot` where you want to add your text (refer to the *How it works...* section for more information on `ggplot2` plots):

   ```
   plot <- ggplot(data = iris, aes(x = Sepal.Length, y =        Sepal.
   Width)) +
      geom_point()
   plot
   ```

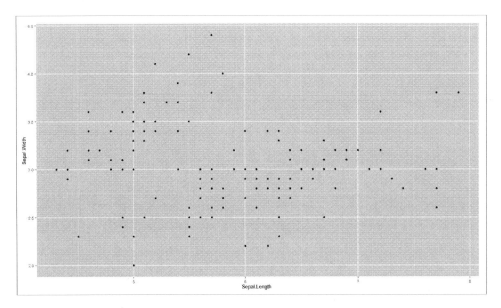

2. Define the text that is to be added:

   ```
   text      <- "there are some cool correlations here"
   ```

3. Select where to enter text:

   ```
   location <- gglocator(1, xexpand = c(0,0), yexpand = c(0,0))
   ```

   Running this code will result in a small pointer appearing on the plot area within the RStudio viewer pane, like the one shown here:

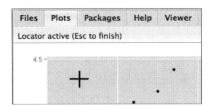

After selecting a point within the plot area, the `location` object will have two attributes:

- ❑ *x* coordinate
- ❑ *y* coordinate

You can easily see them by running `location` within your R console.

4. Add text to the plot:

```
plot +
scale_x_continuous(expand = c(0,0)) +
scale_y_continuous(expand = c(0,0)) +
geom_text(aes(x = location[[1]],y = location[[2]],label= text))
```

5. Change the text color.

```
plot +
  scale_x_continuous(expand = c(0,0)) +
  scale_y_continuous(expand = c(0,0)) +
  geom_text(aes(x = location[[1]],y = location[[2]],label=
text),colour = "red")
```

6. Change the text dimensions:

```
plot +
  scale_x_continuous(expand = c(0,0)) +
  scale_y_continuous(expand = c(0,0)) +
  geom_text(aes(x = location[[1]],y = location[[2]],label=
text),colour = "red",size = 7)
```

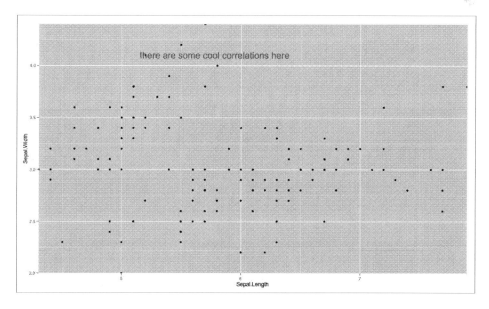

How it works...

Step 1 requires you to create a `ggplot`, which is a plot based on the grammar of graphics.

An extensive introduction to the grammar of graphics and its implementation in the `ggplot2` package is outside the scope of this book. For the grammar of graphics, you can refer to *The Grammar of Graphics* by Leland Wilkinson (`http://www.springer.com/us/book/9780387245447`), which is the foundation of this data visualization theory.

Talking about `ggplot2`, even though the Web is full of articles and tutorials about the usage of this package, I would rather suggest reading the original paper, *A Layered Grammar of Graphics* by our dear Hadley Wickham (`http://byrneslab.net/classes/biol607/readings/wickham_layered-grammar.pdf`); this is what everything started from.

For our purposes, we can just say that every `ggplot` must be composed at least of these three layers:

▶ Data, which means a specification where to look for data to be plotted

▶ Mapping/aesthetics, containing specifications of the *x* and *y* variables (mandatory) and aesthetic parameters (optional)

▶ Geometric objects, which are the actual object representing points defined as couples of *x* and *y*.

Let's look at an example based on the following data frame:

```
dataset <- data.frame(independent = seq(1:3),dependent = seq(4:6))
```

Now, we can define the first layer using the `ggplot()` function, as follows:

```
ggplot(data = dataset, aes(x = independent,y = dependent))+
```

Finally, as the + symbol suggests, we can add the geometric layer:

```
geom_point()
```

Summing up all:

```
ggplot(data = dataset, aes(x = independent,y = dependent))+ geom_
point()
```

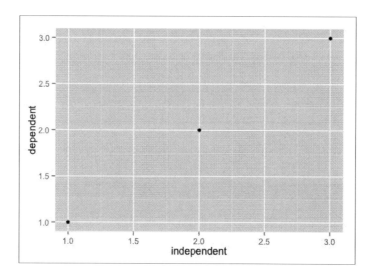

This is the base of every ggplot2 plot. Starting from this point, it is possible to build infinite types of predefined and even customized plots, adding layer over layer.

In our example, we define a basic ggplot mapping to the Sepal.Length and Sepal. Width variables from the Iris dataset.

In step 2, we define the text we want to add to the ggplot plot and assign it to a text object, which is a string vector.

Step 3 leverages gglocator(), a function provided by the ggmap package, which is intended to work as an equivalent of the locator() function for the plot() function. After clicking with the crossed cursor on a point on the plot, the location object will be populated by x and y space coordinates, which will then be used as a reference for custom text placement.

In step 4, we reproduce our base plot by scaling it through scale_x_continuos() and scale_y_continuos() to ensure that the origins of the axes are plotted. These two functions actually define a new layer within our ggplot, namely a scale layer specifying the scale for this plot.

This is needed in order to ensure comparability between plot coordinates and the coordinates stored within the location object, setting all to the point(x = 0, y = 0) at the origin.

Finally, we add the text using the geom_text() function.

This function, in case you are wondering what it does, adds another layer to the plot containing the specified text.

The geom_text() function requires you to specify the text to be placed as an annotation through the argument label, and the *x* and *y* coordinates to be passed within the aes argument, as seen in step 1. While the text is passed through the text object, the last two parameters are set to extract from the location object attributes x and y.

Be aware that not passing x and y, and generally the aes argument, will result in geom_text() looking within the aestethics arguments passed within the ggplot() call.

This will result in text being printed on every point of your plot, as if it were a label of your data.

In step 5, the text color can be changed through the colour parameter within the geom_text() function.

If you want to get an idea of the colors you can use, you should take a look at the minimalist but rather great document *Colors in R* (http://www.stat.columbia.edu/~tzheng/files/Rcolor.pdf), which shows all the tonalities available in base R.

For more advanced color settings, I suggest the RColorBrewer package (https://cran.r-project.org/web/packages/RColorBrewer/index.html). This is based on the Color Brewer project, a really interesting initiative about colors in cartography developed by Cynthia Brewer. You can get to know more about the project at http://colorbrewer2.org/.

You can also change the size of the text using the size argument.

There's more...

In the help documentation for the geom_text() function, you will find that other aesthetic parameters such as text font or text angulation can be set. You can take a look at the documentation in the help tab of your RStudio IDE by running the following:

```
?geom_text
```

Changing axes appearance to ggplot2 plot (continous axes)

This recipe shows you how to get control over an axis within a ggplot plot.

The ggplot2 package does a great job of automatically setting the appearance of the axes, but sometimes, even in the early stages of your project, you may want your axis to appear in a specific shape, showing, for instance, a defined number of tickmarks.

This is what this recipe is all about—giving you control over the appearance of your `ggplot` axes.

In this example, we will use a plot based on the Iris dataset.

The Iris dataset is one of most used datasets in R tutorials and learning sessions, and it is derived from a 1936 paper by Ronald Fisher, named *The use of multiple measurements in taxonomic problems*.

Data was observed on 50 samples of three species of the iris flower:

- Iris setosa
- Iris virginica
- Iris versicolor

On each sample for features were recorded:

- length of the sepals
- width of the sepals
- length of the petals
- width of the petals

For a general and brief introduction to `ggplot` plots, take a look at the *How it works...* section of the previous recipe.

Getting ready

The first step needed to get started with this recipe is `ggplot2` package installation and loading:

```
install.packages("ggplot2")
library(ggplot2)
```

After doing that, we will be able to create a `ggplot2` plot to work on in this recipe:

```
plot <- ggplot(data = iris, aes(x = Sepal.Length, y = Sepal.Width)) +
    geom_point()
```

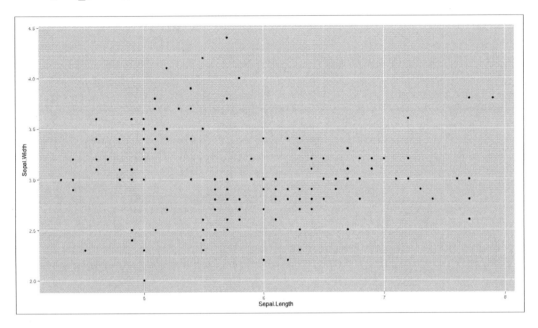

How to do it...

1. Set axis range from 0 to 10.

    Using the `expand_limits()` function, we can set the origin and the end of the *x* and *y* axes, passing these values in two different vectors, one for the *x* and one for the *y* argument of the `expand_limits()` function:

    ```
    plot <- plot + expand_limits(x = c(0,10),y = c(0,10))
    ```

This will result in setting the range of the *x* and *y* axes from 0 to 10.

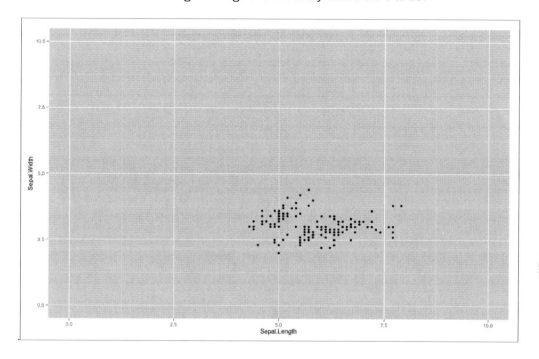

By displaying predetermined tick marks, `ggplot` automatically defines a convenient number of tick marks, working this out with its own internal algorithms. However, you can force the plot to have a custom number of algorithms using the `scale_y_continuos()` and `scale_x_continuos()` functions, passing a vector with the desired breaks to the `breaks` argument:

```
plot <- plot + scale_y_continuous(breaks = c(0,5,10))
```

This piece of code, for instance, will result in a plot having tick marks only on 0, 5, and 10:

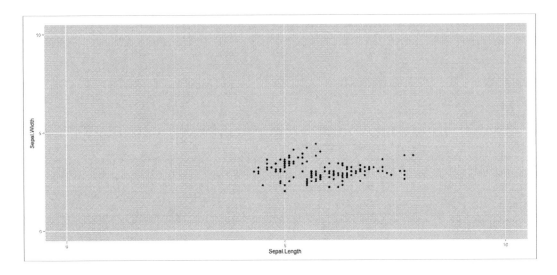

2. Hide the tick marks:

```
plot <- plot + scale_y_continuous(breaks = NULL) + scale_x_
continuous(breaks = NULL)
```

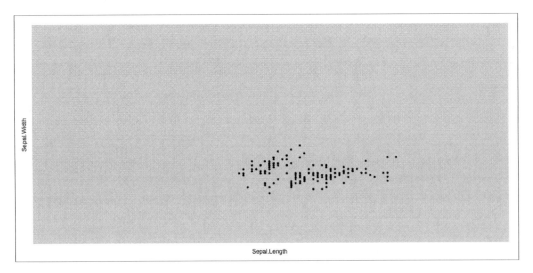

3. Set a fixed ratio between *x* and *y* axes:

```
plot <- plot + coord_fixed(ratio = 4/3)
```

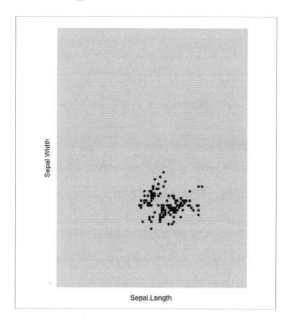

It feels like some kind of pop art, doesn't it?

So, you are now a `ggplot` artist, congratulations!

Producing a matrix of graphs with ggplot2

Sometimes it is useful to display your plots next to one another. This recipe lets you do this by leveraging the `facet_grid()` function in the `ggplot2` package.

Getting ready

The example we will cover in this recipe will require us to apply functions from the `ggplot2` package, and we will therefore have to install and load this package.

Moreover, we will use functions from the `rio` and `tidyr` package in this section.

Let's install and load these packages before moving on:

```
install.packages(c("ggplot2","tidyr","rio"))
library(tidyr)
library(rio)
library(ggplot2)
```

Once we are done with all the installing and loading, we can build the dataset that will be employed in this example.

This dataset is actually a composed one, that is, it is made by merging two different datasets provided by the World Bank.

This institution produces a really great number of dataset packed with metadata and convenient download facilities at the following website:

`http://data.worldbank.org`

As discussed, we will merge two different datasets, one recording life expectancy by country from the year 1960 to 2015, and the other recording population for the same countries and the same period.

But now it is time to get our dataset ready.

We will start with importing raw data from two separate `.xlsx` files (you can choose different formats from the website) that are provided in the RStudio project related to this book.

You can download it by authenticating your account at `http://packtpub.com`.

The data loading task will be accomplished using the powerful `import()` function from the `rio` package. If you want to know more on this, refer to the *Loading data into R with rio packages* recipe from *Chapter 1, Acquiring Data for Your Project*.

Here is the script:

```
population <- import("population_by_country.xlsx")
expectancy <- import("expentancy_by_country.xlsx")
```

As you can see after running `View()` on these data frames, both of them have one country for each row and one year for each column.

Since these datasets contain too many countries and years to be plotted all at once, we will now filter rows and column to retain only eight countries and six years.

The following are the chosen countries:

- ▸ Germany
- ▸ Greece
- ▸ Singapore
- ▸ Sweden
- ▸ Tajikistan
- ▸ United States
- ▸ Zambia
- ▸ Zimbabwe

The chosen years are 1968, 1978, 1988, 1998, and 2998:

```
population <- population[c(53,85,212,234),1:10]
expectancy <- expectancy[c(53,85,212,234),1:10]
```

We also want to add a `continent` variable to be used as a faceting variable, meaning a variable against which to plot population and expectancy variables:

```
population <- data.frame("continent" =          c("Europe","Europe","A
sia","Europe","Asia","North_America","Africa","Africa"),population)
expectancy <- data.frame("continent" = c("Europe","Europe","Asia","Eur
ope","Asia","North_America","Africa","Africa"),expectancy)
```

Since both data frames are in a form not really convenient for our visualization, we are now going to apply the `gather()` function to them to change their structures and make them fit a more tidy form, where each row corresponds to an observation:

```
population_tidy <- gather(population,year,population,3:ncol(populati
on))
expectancy_tidy <- gather(expectancy,year,expectancy,3:ncol(expectan
cy))
```

The `gather()` function is covered in great detail in *Chapter 2, Preparing for Analysis – Data Cleansing and Manipulation*, in the *Preparing your data for analysis with the tidyr package* recipe.

We are nearly done; just take a second to change column names before merging datasets:

```
colnames(population_tidy) <- c("continent","country","year","populati
on")
colnames(expectancy_tidy) <- c("continent","country","year","expectan
cy")
```

It is now time to actually merge the two datasets, specifying which column will be used as a key:

```
dataset <- merge(population_tidy,expectancy_tidy,by =
c("continent","country", "year"))
```

Now that we are done with this warm up, we can go on to plot our data.

How to do it...

1. Plot your data.

   Let's plot our data in a basic `ggplot` plot, where *x* denotes life expectancy and *y* denotes population. Here, we will not distinguish between countries:

   ```
   plot <- ggplot(data = dataset, aes(x = expectancy, y =
   population)) +
   geom_point()+
     ggtitle("life expectancy against population")
   plot
   ```

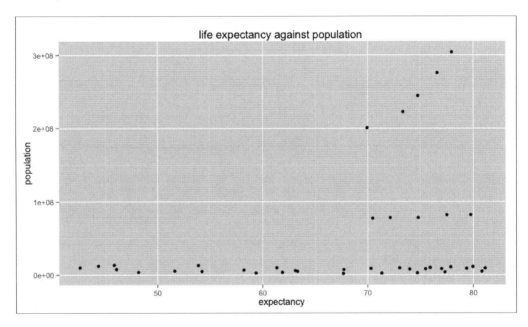

   Here comes a little quiz for you. How would you assign country names to these groups of points within the plot?

   Obviously, you don't have to worry; you will find the answer below.

2. Add a first facet to plot your variables aggregated by country. Here is the answer:

```
plot_by_country <- plot + facet_grid(. ~ country)+
    ggtitle("life expectancy against population by country")
plot_by_country
```

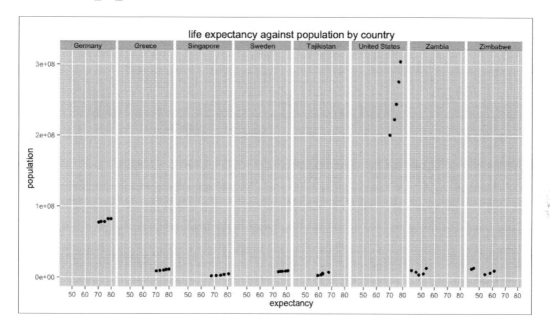

Did you get all the countries right? Good, as you can see, faceting lets us easily distinguish between different series of data within the dataset, and we can immediately make sense.

Now, we will add another facet using the `continent` variable.

3. Add a second facet using the `continent` variable.

    This requires you to specify a second argument within the `facet_grid()` function:

    ```
    plot_by_continent <- plot_by_country + facet_grid(continent ~
    country) +
      ggtitle("life expectancy against population by continent by
    country")
    plot_by_continent
    ```

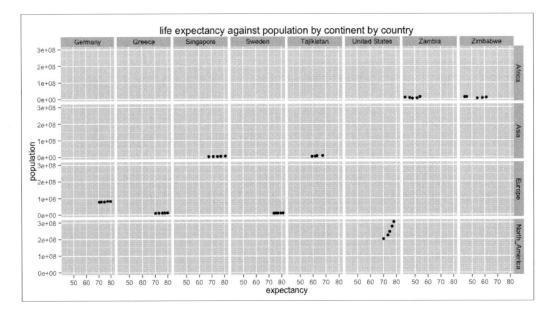

How it works...

Step 1 requires you to produce a first basic `ggplot` plot composed of data specification and variable mapping, along with a `geom_point()` layer used to plot the specified variables against one an other.

You can find out more about the `ggplot` logic by reading the *How it works...* section of the *Adding text to a ggplot2 plot at a custom location* recipe.

In step 2, in order to understand the `facet_grid()` mechanism, we need to think about the dataset behind the plot we are showing off.

Our complete dataset is composed of 40 observations of 5 attributes, namely `continent`, `country`, `year`, `population`, and `expectancy`. These 40 observations can be divided into 8 subdatasets, considering that they come from 40 observations from eight different countries.

This division is exactly what the `facet_grid(~ country)` function does:

▸ Splits the `dataset` data frame into eight subdata frames (one for each country)

▸ Plots those data frames separately, following the indication given when initializing the plot object (that is, `aes(x =population, y =expectancy)`)

Step 3 talks about adding variables. This step is an incremental step. If we divide our iris data frame by country within the previous one, obtaining 8 smaller data frames with this step, we take this process further by dividing our 8 data frames by continent, obtaining 24 subdata data frames:

*4 possibile values for continent * 4 possible values for country = 24*

The resultant plot is obtained by putting together all the singular plots of those data frames, obtained following the `aes()` parameter provided to plot objects.

Drawing a route on a map with ggmap

Working with geospatial data is a simple task with R. Thankfully, the `ggmap` package provides a good number of facilities for this task.

In particular, this recipe gives you the ability to draw on a map a custom defined route from one point to another.

Getting ready

As you can imagine, we first need to install and load the `ggmap` package:

```
install.packages("ggmap")
library(ggmap)
```

How to do it...

1. Define the route points using the `route()` function:

```
trip        <- (route(from = "rome", to = "milan",structure =
"route", output = "simple"))
```

2. Create the map where you want to draw the route:

```
route_map <- get_map("italy",zoom = 6)
```

3. Define the `segment` and `segment_couple` variables to link trip points:

```
segment <- c()
for(i in 1:nrow(trip)){
   if(i == 1){segment[i] <- 1}else{
```

```
      if( i %% 2 != 0 ){
        segment [i] <- i-segment[i-1]}else{
          segment [i] <- i/2
        }
    }
}
segment_couple <- c(0,segment[-length(segment)])
trip$segment <- segment
trip$segment_couple <- segment_coupleDraw the final map
route_map +
  geom_point(aes(x = lon, y = lat, size = 5, colour = hours),data
= trip)+
geom_line(data = trip,aes(group = segment)) +
  geom_line(data = trip, aes(group = segment_couple))
```

This code will result in the following map being plotted within the viewer pane (Reference: Map data 2015 GeoBasis-De/BKG):

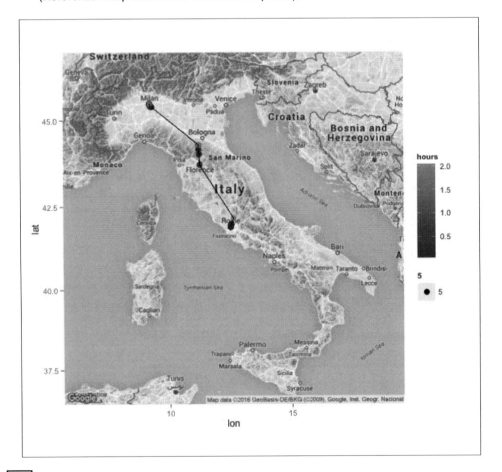

How it works...

In step 1, we define route points using the `route()` function. The `route()` function queries the Google Maps server to retrieve a set of points describing the requested route. Since we specified `output = "simple"`, the output will result in `data.frame` with the following attributes:

```
$ m          : num   15 49 66 124 157 173 546 139 393 243 ...
 $ km         : num   0.015 0.049 0.066 0.124 0.157 0.173 0.546 0.139
0.393 0.243 ...
  $ miles     : num   0.00932 0.03045 0.04101 0.07705 0.09756 ...
  $ seconds   : num   3 25 26 20 34 44 134 37 75 45 ...
  $ minutes   : num   0.05 0.417 0.433 0.333 0.567 ...
  $ hours     : num   0.000833 0.006944 0.007222 0.005556 0.009444 ...
  $ leg       : int   1 2 3 4 5 6 7 8 9 10 ...
  $ lon       : num   12.5 12.5 12.5 12.5 12.5 ...
  $ lat       : num   41.9 41.9 41.9 41.9 41.9 ...
```

Here are all possible arguments to be specified when calling the function:

Argument	Description
`from`	This is the name of the origin address in a data frame (vector accepted).
`to`	This is the name of the destination address in a data frame (vector accepted).
`mode`	This can be driving, cycling, walking, or transit.
`structure`	This is the structure of the output (refer to examples).
`output`	This is the amount of output.
`alternatives`	This answers the question, "should more than one route be provided?"
`messaging`	This turns the messaging on or off.
`sensor`	This states whether or not the geocoding request comes from a device with a location sensor.
`override_limit`	This overrides the current query count (`.GoogleRouteQueryCount`).

In step 2, we define the `segment` and `segment_couple` variables to link trip points. Custom route visualization will be obtained by leveraging the `geom_line()` function and passing to it a `group` argument in order to link adjacent points in the route (refer to the details of step 3 for further info rmation).

This can be done only after having defined the segment and segment_couple variables, which are basically a way to link two points stored in two subsequent points, giving them a common value for the segment and segment_couple variables.

Here is how it looks (only last columns are shown here):

```
> head(trip[,8:11])
        lon      lat segment segment_couple
1 12.49640 41.90290       1              0
2 12.49623 41.90293       1              1
3 12.49573 41.90318       2              1
4 12.49600 41.90359       2              2
5 12.49710 41.90434       3              2
6 12.49587 41.90541       3              3
```

As you can easily see, every point is linked to the precedent by the segment variable and is linked to the subsequent by the segment_couple variable.

We draw the final map in step 3. This step involves the following:

- The creation of a route_map object through the get_map function, which produces another query to the Google Maps server
- The plotting of this map, consisting of points and lines

Points are obtained using the geom_point() function and passing to it lon and lat as x and y, while lines are obtained with two calls to the geom_line() function, the first having the segment variable as the grouping factor (that is, the rule you use to draw lines on your plot) and the second having the segment_couple variable as the grouping factor. Through this double call, we can be sure that every point is connected to each other.

See also

- You can find out more about ggmap in the introductory paper *ggmap: Spatial Visualization with ggplot2* (http://vita.had.co.nz/papers/ggmap.html).

Making use of the igraph package to draw a network

The igraph package is a reference point for network visualization in the R environment.

igraph is actually more than an R package, since you can use igraph tools even with Python and C/C++.

If you are performing analysis that involves network visualizations and R, you should look at this package as one of your more relevant allies.

This recipe will let you enter the wide world of network visualization with R, showing you how to create a network plot starting from a data frame.

Getting ready

Install the `igraph` package:

```
install.packages("igraph")
library(igraph)
```

We will use the `flo` dataset showing the relationship between Renaissance Florentine families.

Marriage between Adimari and Cascioni families, from Cassone Adimari, around 1420, Florence

This dataset is provided as an adjacency matrix within the network package.

Therefore, in order to make it available, we have to install the `network` package and load the dataset by running the `data()` function on it:

```
install.packages("network")
library(network)
data(flo)
```

You can then visualize the `flo` dataset within the RStudio viewer pane by running the `View` command:

```
View(flo)
```

This will result in the following visualization:

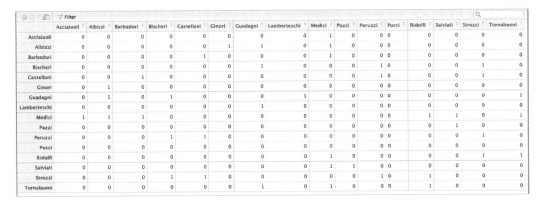

	Accialuoli	Albizzi	Barbadori	Bischeri	Castellani	Ginori	Guadagni	Lamberteschi	Medici	Pazzi	Peruzzi	Pucci	Ridolfi	Salviati	Strozzi	Tornabuoni
Accialuoli	0	0	0	0	0	0	0	0	1	0	0	0	0	0	0	0
Albizzi	0	0	0	0	0	1	1	0	1	0	0	0	0	0	0	0
Barbadori	0	0	0	0	1	0	0	0	1	0	0	0	0	0	0	0
Bischeri	0	0	0	0	0	0	1	0	0	0	1	0	0	0	1	0
Castellani	0	0	1	0	0	0	0	0	0	0	1	0	0	0	1	0
Ginori	0	1	0	0	0	0	0	0	0	0	0	0	0	0	0	0
Guadagni	0	1	0	1	0	0	0	1	0	0	0	0	0	0	0	1
Lamberteschi	0	0	0	0	0	0	1	0	0	0	0	0	0	0	0	0
Medici	1	1	1	0	0	0	0	0	0	0	0	0	1	1	0	1
Pazzi	0	0	0	0	0	0	0	0	0	0	0	0	0	1	0	0
Peruzzi	0	0	0	1	1	0	0	0	0	0	0	0	0	0	1	0
Pucci	0	0	0	0	0	0	0	0	0	0	0	0	0	0	0	0
Ridolfi	0	0	0	0	0	0	0	0	1	0	0	0	0	0	1	1
Salviati	0	0	0	0	0	0	0	0	1	1	0	0	0	0	0	0
Strozzi	0	0	0	1	1	0	0	0	0	0	1	0	1	0	0	0
Tornabuoni	0	0	0	0	0	0	1	0	1	0	0	0	1	0	0	0

This dataset is actually an adjacency matrix, where 0 at the I, J cell expresses no relationship between the i-esim and the j-esim families, while 1 represents evidence of a relationship.

For instance, we can assume from the matrix that some kind of relationship exists between the Albizzi and the Tornabuoni family. I am guessing you are curious, so I will let you know what this relationship is.

At the age of 18, on June 15, 1486, Giovanna Albizzi linked her family to one of the Tornabuonis by marrying Lorenzo Tornabuoni. Was it true love?

Ok, I think you are getting too curious now...

> Be aware that this recipe can be applied even having as an input and hedge list, simply by substituting steps 1 and 2 with a single step where the hedge list is passed as an argument to the graph.data.frame() function.

How to do it...

1. Create a matrix object from the flo dataset:

   ```
   dataset <- as.matrix(flo)
   ```

2. Create an igraph object from the defined dataset:

   ```
   net    <- graph.adjacency(dataset,mode = "undirected", weighted =
   NULL)
   ```

3. Compute the degree of each vertex:

   ```
   deg <- degree(net, mode = "all")
   ```

4. Set the size of each vertex equal to its degree:

   ```
   V(net)$size <- deg*4
   ```

5. Set the arrow size:

   ```
   E(net)$arrow.size <- .2
   ```

6. Set the color of the edges:

   ```
   E(net)$edge.color <- "gray"
   ```

7. Plot your network:

   ```
   plot(net)
   ```

   You will then see the following plot:

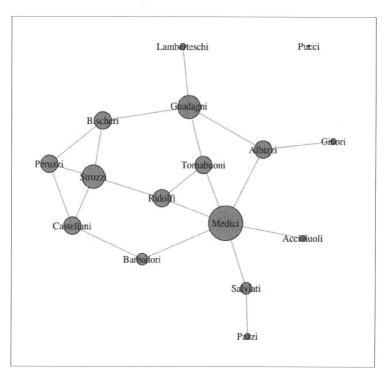

How it works...

In step 1, we create a `matrix` object from the `flo` dataset. The `graph.adjacency()` function requires you to pass to it a `matrix` object in order to create an `igrpah` object. Therefore, we cast our data frames into a `matrix` object, leveraging the `as.matrix()` function.

Then in step 2, we create an `igraph` object from the defined dataset. Creating an `igraph` object is necessary in order to make use of all the great utilities made available through the `igraph` package.

In this case, since we are working on an `adjacency` matrix, we will obtain this through the `graph.adjacency()` function. This function takes as an input an adjacency matrix and gives as an output an `igraph` object.

In step 3, we compute the degree of each vertex. The **degree** is a matrix associated to every node of a network. It basically measures the number of edges connected to that node.

To begin with, it is a convenient way to measure the relevance of a node in a network. Why? To answer this question, I will let you take a look at the Medici node.

How many connections did the Medici family have? Six connections, which is the maximum number in the matrix. As you may know (if not, go to `https://en.wikipedia.org/wiki/House_of_Medici`), the Medici were one of the most influent and powerful families of the Italian Renaissance period, and the degree computed for this family accurately reflected this reality.

We measure the degree of each node just by calling the `degree()` function on the `net` object.

Next, in step 4 we set the size of each vertex equal to its degree. We now set the value of an attribute of our network vertex (node). In particular, we set the node size, and this attribute is set equal to the previously computed degree for each node.

As you would expect if you have not skipped the explanation in the previous step, the Medici family is the one represented by the largest node. Note that using the same syntax, other attributes can be added or set to vertexes and to edges as well (as you can see in the next steps).

In step 5, we set the arrow size. In a way similar to what we have done with nodes, we now set the size of the edges. In this case, we set it to a fixed number, but we can even set it as a function of some other network parameter.

In step 6, we set the color of the edges. In this step, the edge color attribute is set to grey.

Lastly, in step 7 we plot our network. Plotting an `igraph` object is really straightforward, requiring you to only run the base R `plot()` function. As seen in the *Looking at your data using the plot() function* recipe, this function is able to change its output depending on the class of data given as input, thanks to specific methods that enrich the function's capabilities for a given kind of object. Refer to the cited recipe for further information on this function, but in the meanwhile, appreciate the result of your efforts!

Showing communities in a network with the linkcomm package

The linkcomm package is an R package developed with the main aim of letting you discover and study communities that exist within your network. These communities are discovered by applying an algorithm derived from the paper *Link communities reveal multiscale complexity in networks* by *Ahn Y.Y., Bagrow J.P., and Lehmann.*

Getting ready

In order to use `linkcomm` functionalities, we first need to install and load the `linkcomm` package:

```
install.packages("linkcomm")
library(linkcomm)
```

As a sample dataset, we will use the `lesmiserables` hedge list, provided in the `linkcomm` package. This dataset basically shows relations hips between characters in Victor Hugo's novel *Les Misérables*.

You can get a sense of the dataset by running `str()` on it:

```
> str(lesmiserables)
'data.frame':  254 obs. of  2 variables:
 $ V1: Factor w/ 73 levels "Anzelma","Babet",..: 61 49 55 55 21 33 12 23
20 62 ...
 $ V2: Factor w/ 49 levels "Babet","Bahorel",..: 42 42 42 36 42 42 42 42
42 42 ...
```

How to do it...

1. Create a `linkcomm` object:

   ```
   linkcomm_object <- getLinkCommunities(lesmiserables, hcmethod =
   "single")
   ```

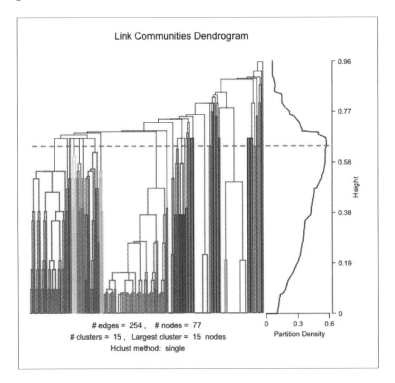

2. Show network with communities:

   ```
   plot(linkcom_obj, type = "graph", layout = layout.fruchterman.
   reingold)
   ```

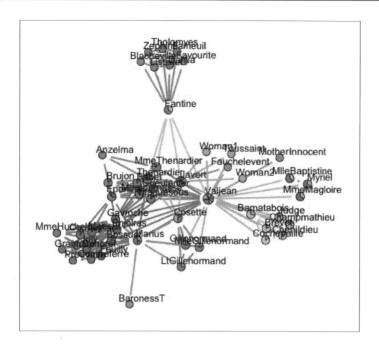

3. Select the nodes to be displayed:

```
plot(linkcom_obj, type = "graph", layout = "spencer.circle",
shownodesin = 3)
```

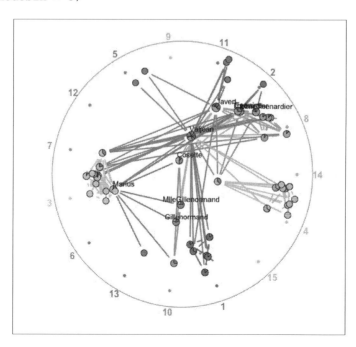

4. Show the composition of the communities:

```
plot(linkcom_obj, type = "members")
```

This plot shows members and the community that they belong to:

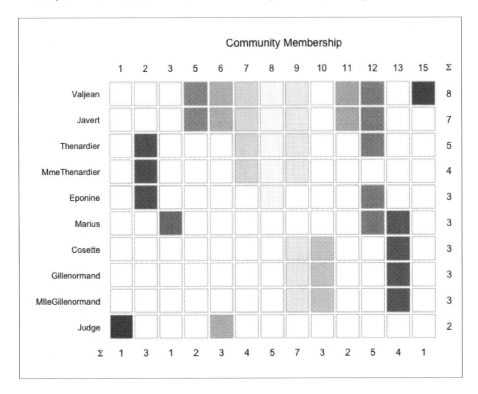

How it works...

In step 1, we create a `linkcomm` object. The `linkcomm` objects are, as you have probably guessed, the base components of every network visualization within the `linkcomm` package. These objects are characterized as a list object, storing relevant attributes for the given network.

It is interesting to note that `linkcomm` objects are built on the base of an `igraph` object, confirming the relevance of the latter package for network visualization in R.

What `linkcomm` adds to the `igraph` object is information about communities that exist within the network. These communities are derived by applying the cited algorithm on the hedge list provided. This is a good example of how the R community is able into begin the language development starting from what of good has already been done.

This algorithm basically looks for nodes that have a good enough number of common links and can be considered as clustering algorithms, as made clear by the dendogram that appears once `getLinkCommunities()` is executed.

In step 2, we show the network with communities. This step once again makes use of the `plot()` function's flexibility. As seen in the *Looking at your data using the plot() function* recipe, this function is able to change its output depending on the class of the data given as input. Refer to cited recipe for further information on this function.

Also note that it is possible to change the layout of your plot by modifying the layout argument in the `plot()` function.

Here are the available layouts:

- `spencer.circle`
- `layout.random`
- `layout.circle`
- `layout.sphere`
- `layout.fruchterman.reingold`
- `layout.kamada.kawai`
- `layout.spring`
- `layout.reingold.tilford`
- `layout.fruchterman.reingold.grid`
- `layout.lgl`
- `layout.graphopt`
- `layout.mds`
- `layout.svd`
- `layout.norm`

Next, in step 3 we select the nodes to be displayed. When working with large networks, having the possibility to focus your attention on just a selection of them is a really useful feature. The `linkcomm` package implements this feature through the `shownodesin` argument in the plot function. This parameter lets you virtually filter your nodes, highlighting only nodes pertaining to at least *n* communities, where *n* is a custom number having as a maximum the total number of identified communities.

Lastly, in step 4 we show the composition of the communities. The plot displayed in step 4 is a really useful visualization of our network, since it lets you easily analyze the composition of the communities. I hope that looking at these Les Misérables. character links will make you willing to read the great novel by Victor Hugo, or at least watch the movie!

4

Advanced and Interactive Visualization

In this chapter, we will cover the following recipes:

- ▶ Producing a Sankey diagram with the `networkD3` package
- ▶ Creating a dynamic force network with the `visNetwork` package
- ▶ Building a rotating 3D graph and exporting it as a GIF
- ▶ Using the `DiagrammeR` package to produce a process flow diagram in RStudio

Introduction

A legendary tale says that Michelangelo found his Moses so real; and shouted at him "Why don't you speak?!" Seeing that it wouldn't, he slammed it down with his hammer.

Michelangelo's Mosè. Picture by Jörg Bittner Unna, CC BY 3.0,
`https://commons.wikimedia.org/w/index.php?curid=46476418`

From a similar desire of interaction, interactive visualization was born, making your data visualizations interact with you and your analysis users.

Using interactive visualizations, we can make our plots do something more than just displaying data, since we give them the ability to interact with the user, showing tooltips, navigation, and zooming controls, and even rearranging them according to users' needs and preferences.

Interactive data visualization can be useful at the beginning and at the end of your work.

At the beginning, in your exploratory data analysis job, you can leverage interactive visualizations in order to get a better understanding of your data without needing to write a lot of code for a great number of plots.

At the end of your job, you can use interactive data visualization to better communicate your point, by showing your assumptions and their effects on your job results in a better manner.

In this chapter, you will learn some advanced techniques to produce interactive data visualization, from force networks to animated 3D plots.

Producing a Sankey diagram with the networkD3 package

A Sankey diagram is a really powerful way of displaying your data. Particularly, Sankey diagrams are a really convenient way of showing flows of data from their origin to their end.

A really famous example of these kind of diagrams is the one presented by Charles Minard's 1869 chart showing the number of men in Napoleon's 1812 Russian campaign army, their movements, as well as the temperature they encountered on the return path:

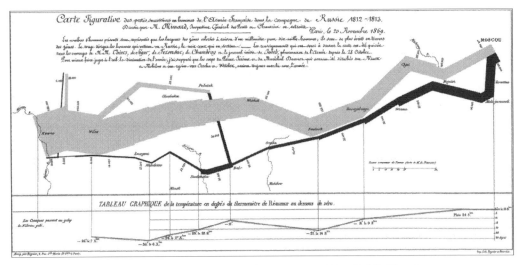

Source: https://en.wikipedia.org/wiki/Sankey_diagram#/media/File:Minard.png

In a Sankey diagram, a given amount is shown on the leftmost side of the plot and, while moving to the right (which can be interpreted as the flow of time), this given amount is split into parts or simply reduced. The latter is the case for the Minard's diagram, where soldiers died during the campaign and the number of deaths are counted in a separate line plot at the bottom.

Getting ready

In order to get started with this recipe, you will need to install and load the `networkD3` and `jsonlite` packages:

```
install.packages(c("networkD3","jsonlite"))
library(networkD3)
library(jsonlite)
```

The first package is the one which implements the `sankeyNetwork()` function that we will leverage in our recipe, while the second one is simply required to parse the dataset we will use from the JSON format to the data frame.

Our example will regard energy flow from production to the final usage or waste, using the original dataset provided by Christopher Gandrud, creator of the `networkD3` package.

In order to make this dataset available, we first need to download it and then convert it from `jsonlite` to an ordinary list:

1. Define a `URL` object pointing to the data source:

    ```
    URL <- paste0
    ("https://cdn.rawgit.com/christophergandrud/networkD3/",
        "master/JSONdata/energy.json")
    ```

2. Define an `Energy` object where we can store the data from the defined source:

    ```
    Energy <- jsonlite::fromJSON(URL)
    ```

This `Energy` list will now be composed by two data frames; one for nodes (that is, vertex) and one for links (that is, edges):

```
List of 2
 $ nodes:'data.frame': 48 obs. of  1 variable:
  ..$ name: chr [1:48] "Agricultural 'waste'" "Bio-conversion" "Liquid"
"Losses" ...
 $ links:'data.frame': 68 obs. of  3 variables:
  ..$ source: int [1:68] 0 1 1 1 1 6 7 8 10 9 ...
  ..$ target: int [1:68] 1 2 3 4 5 2 4 9 9 4 ...
  ..$ value : num [1:68] 124.729 0.597 26.862 280.322 81.144 …
```

The latter data frame is a list of weighted hedges, where a starting point and an end point are exposed, and this link is weighted by a value attribute.

If you are willing to apply this recipe to your data, which I hope you are, you should have them arranged within two distinct data frames with the following structure:

- The nodes data frame:

    - **Nodes**: This is a vector of all your nodes' names, with no duplications

- The links data frame:

    - **From**: This is a numeric column showing the first node of every connection in your diagram. Let's say that if you want to introduce a connection between the first and the third nodes defined with Nodes, you should write 0 here (and 3 within the to argument) as shown in this example; be aware that first node has value 0 and not 1

    - **To**: This is a numeric column showing the end of every connection in your diagram

    - **Weight**: This is the value of your connection, meaning how much of your flow passes through this connection

It may be useful to you to underline that the second data frame is rightly named a hedge list, where each observation represents a hedge of your network.

How to do it...

1. Produce the Sankey diagram, as follows:

```
sankeyNetwork(Links = Energy$links, Nodes = Energy$nodes,
Source = "source",
   Target = "target", Value = "value", NodeID = "name",
   units = "TWh", fontSize = 12, nodeWidth = 30)
```

This will result in the following Sankey diagram:

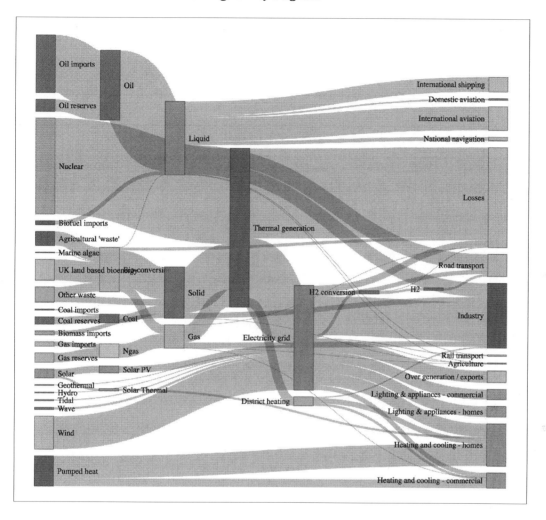

2. We will now adjust the font size by changing the value of the `fontSize` parameter:

```
sankeyNetwork(Links = Energy$links, Nodes = Energy$nodes,
Source = "source",
  Target = "target", Value = "value", NodeID = "name",
  units = "TWh", fontSize = 10, nodeWidth = 30)
```

3. Next, we change `nodeWidth`:

```
sankeyNetwork(Links = Energy$links, Nodes = Energy$nodes,
Source = "source",
  Target = "target", Value = "value", NodeID = "name",
  units = "TWh", fontSize = 12, nodeWidth = 5)
```

4. In order to embed your Sankey diagram, you can leverage the RStudio **Save as Web Page** control from the **Export** menu:

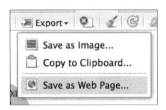

This control will let you save your diagram as an HTML file.

How it works...

In step 1 we call the `sankeyNetwork()` function, which will produce an interactive Sankey diagram in your RStudio Viewer pane, where the node alignment can be customized and flows can be highlighted by clicking on them.

In step 4 we save your Sankey diagram as a web page, which will let you embed on websites, preserving interactive features.

Creating a dynamic force network with the visNetwork package

The `visNetwork` package is one among the most popular packages in the R community, mainly because it lets you display networks and interact with them without having to invest too much time.

This recipe will get you up and running with this package, showing you all that you need to know to start exploring your network in a fully interactive way.

Getting ready

In order to get started with this recipe, you will need to install and load the `visNetwork` package to actually produce your network visualizations.

We will also use the `jsonlite` package to parse the dataset we will use from the JSON format to the data frame:

```
install.packages(c("visnetwork","jsonlite"))
library(visnetwork)
library(jsonlite)
```

How to do it...

1. Download the dataset from the Web and assign it to the `Energy` object:

```
URL <- paste0
("https://cdn.rawgit.com/christophergandrud/networkD3/",
  "master/JSONdata/energy.json")
Energy <- jsonlite::fromJSON(URL)
```

2. Now create the `nodes` object:

```
nodes <- data.frame(label = Energy$nodes$name , id =
1:length(Energy$nodes$name))
```

3. Create the `edges` object:

```
edges <- data.frame( from = Energy$links$source,
  to = Energy$links$target,
  value = Energy$links$value)
```

4. Next, visualize the network:

    ```
    visNetwork(nodes,edges)
    ```

    This will result in the following interactive visualization:

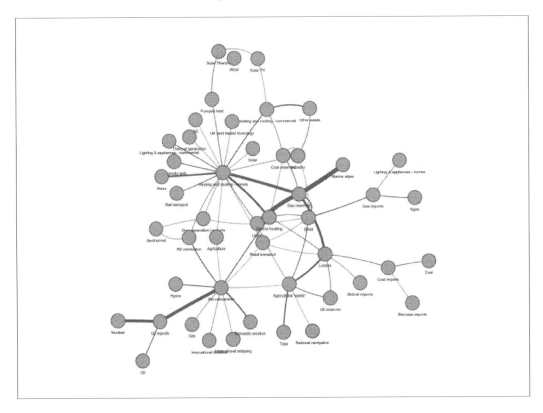

5. Add explicative tooltips to your edges:

    ```
    edges <- data.frame( from = Energy$links$source,
       to = Energy$links$target,
       value = Energy$links$value,
       title = paste0("flow = ", Energy$links$value))
    ```

    This will make the following tooltip appear when hovering over the edge.color:

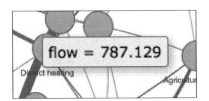

6. Next, we will add a legend to the plot.

    Adding a legend will require you to introduce groups in your data. Therefore, we will need to modify the `nodes` object:

    ```
    nodes <- data.frame(label = Energy$nodes$name ,
      group = c("Group A", "Group B"),
      id = c(1:length(Energy$nodes$name)))
    ```

    A legend will then be added when you run the following code:

    ```
    visNetwork(nodes,edges) %>%
      visLegend()
    ```

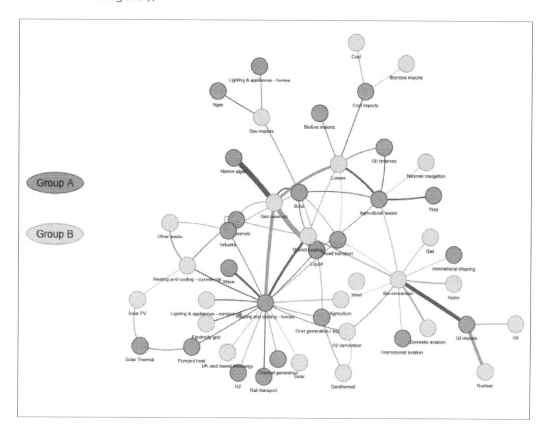

7. We will now add navigation buttons:

   Adding a navigation button requires that you specify the `visInteraction` parameter:

   ```
   visNetwork(nodes,edges) %>%
     visInteraction(navigationButtons = TRUE)
   ```

   Let's take a look at the following image:

How it works...

In step 1 we download the dataset from the Web and assign it to the `Energy` object. The dataset we used shows data for energy flows right from their production to their consumption or waste.

The dataset is composed of a `nodes` data frame and a links `data.frame`, as we can clearly see when we run `str(Energy)`:

```
List of 2
 $ nodes:'data.frame': 48 obs. of  1 variable:
  ..$ name: chr [1:48] "Agricultural 'waste'" "Bio-conversion" "Liquid"
"Losses" ...
 $ links:'data.frame': 68 obs. of  3 variables:
  ..$ source: int [1:68] 0 1 1 1 1 6 7 8 10 9 ...
  ..$ target: int [1:68] 1 2 3 4 5 2 4 9 9 4 ...
  ..$ value : num [1:68] 124.729 0.597 26.862 280.322 81.144 …
```

The `nodes` data frame contains label of our nodes, while the `links` data frame basically contains the connection between our nodes weighted by an amount (value attribute) representing the flow going from one node to another.

To apply this recipe to your data, you should have them arranged in two distinct data frames with the following structure:

► The nodes data frame:

    □ **Nodes**: This is a vector of all your nodes' names, with no duplications

▸ The links data frame:

   ❏ **From**: This is a numeric column showing the first node of every connection in your diagram. Let's say that if you want to introduce a connection between the first and the third nodes defined with `Nodes`, you should write `0` here (and `3` within the to argument) as shown in this example; be aware that first node has value `0` and not `1`

   ❏ **To**: This is a numeric column showing the end of every connection within your diagram

   ❏ **Weight**: This is the value of your connection, meaning how much of your flow passes through this connection

The second data frame is useful for you to underline, in that the second data frame is rightly named hedge list, where each observation represents a hedge of your network.

In step 2 we create `nodes` object. The `nodes` object required by the `visNetwork()` function must be composed of a numeric ID and a character label. That is why we create a nodes `data.frame` using the `name` attribute from the `Energy` object and adding a sequence from `1:length(Energy$nodes$name)` as the IDs.

In step 3 we create the edges object. In a way analogous to what we have done with nodes, we will now create edges for our network, taking data from the links `data.frame` within the `Energy` object.

In step 4 we visualize your network. This is where your data visualization comes to life. Running `visNetwork` on your previously created `visNetwork` object will make an interactive plot showing up in your RStudio viewer pane.

Nodes composing the network can be fully rearranged by dragging and dropping, giving you the possibility to have the clearest possible picture of your data.

This is not exactly like making the Mosè talk, but we are getting closer.

In step 5 we explicative tooltips to your edges. Tooltips are added to the plot, giving a title column within the edges data frame. This attribute will automatically be recognized as a tooltip source by the `visNetwork()` function that we call to visualize our network.

In step 6 we add a legend. The `visLegend()` function is piped into `visInteraction` using the `%>%` operator, which is made available in R by the `magrittR` package that produces a typical command-line pipe functionality into the R language.

In step 7 we add navigation buttons. Especially when dealing with complex and heavily populated networks, adding navigation buttons will be of great help.

These tools will give the ability to zoom in to the plot, making it possible for us to focus on particular communities within the network and fully understand relationships among their members.

There's more...

Since `visNewtork` is a really popular package, you will find plenty of resources if you surf the Web.

Nevertheless, if you are interested in deepening your knowledge about this instrument, I warmly suggest that you look for the official documentation on its website (`http://dataknowledge.github.io/visNetwork/`), which will give you a complete and up-to-date view of its functionalities.

Building a rotating 3D graph and exporting it as a GIF

When dealing with complex datasets, having the possibility to show your data in a 3D environment can be really enhancing.

This recipe will show you how to create such a plot, animate it, and export your animation as a GIF.

Getting ready

This recipe will leverage the `rgl` package specifically developed for 3D visualizations in R:

```
install.packages("rgl")
library(rgl)
```

We will also need to install **ImageMagick** in order to perform the export into the GIF format.

You can find instructions for software installation at `http://www.imagemagick.org/script/binary-releases.php`.

As an explicative dataset, we will use the `iris` dataset, which is a built-in dataset available with all base R installations.

The `iris` dataset is one of the most used datasets in R tutorials and learning sessions, and it is derived from a 1936 paper by Ronald Fisher, named *The use of multiple measurements in taxonomic problems*.

Data was observed on 50 samples of 3 species of the iris flower:

- ▶ Iris setosa
- ▶ Iris virginica
- ▶ Iris versicolor

On each sample, four features were recorded:

- ▶ Length of the sepals
- ▶ Width of the sepals
- ▶ Length of the petals
- ▶ Width of the petals

How to do it...

1. Let's start by creating and visualizing a 3D plot

    The `plot3d()` function lets you easily create and visualize a 3D plot, specifying which data is to be used for each one of three dimensions. The function can be seen as a 3D version of the base R `plot()` function:

    ```
    plot3d(iris$Sepal.Length, iris$Sepal.Width,
    iris$Petal.Length,
      type = "p", col = as.numeric(iris$Species),size = 10)
    ```

    This code will result in the following 3D plot:

    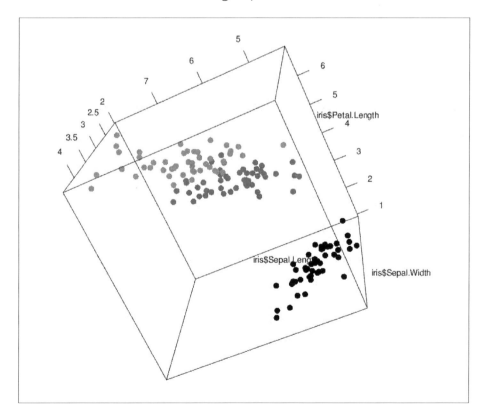

2. Next, we will add a title. In order to add a title, we just have to specify a value for the `main` argument in the `plot3d()` function:

```
plot3d(iris$Sepal.Length, iris$Sepal.Width,
iris$Petal.Length,
   type = "p", col = as.numeric(iris$Species),size = 10,
main = "iris dataset visualization")
```

3. In this step, we will launch a 3D animation. 3D animations can be produced by combining the `spin3d()` and `play3d()` functions, where the first specifies rotation and velocity, and the latter adds a duration argument to set the number of seconds of automatic animation:

```
play3d(spin3d(axis = c(0, 0, 1), rpm = 20), duration = 2)
```

This code will result in the opening of a small window that shows the previously seen plot rotating for two seconds. Beware that by changing the axis parameter, you can change the axis on which the plot will rotate.

4. We can now increment the rotation duration as follows:

```
play3d(spin3d(axis = c(0, 0, 1), rpm = 20), duration = 10)
```

5. In this step, we will export our animation as a GIF. Animation export leverages the `movie3d()` function to which we pass the `spin3d()` function and a duration argument in a way similar to what we have seen for the `play3d()` function:

```
movie3d(spin3d(axis = c(0, 0, 1), rpm = 20),duration = 3,
movie = "the_movie_name_without_extension")
```

As a result, a `.gif` file will be created in your current directory, and it will be named as per the value of the movie argument.

Using the DiagrammeR package to produce a process flow diagram in RStudio

Process flow diagrams are powerful tools for process analysis, and having created a way to produce them in R is one among the greatest credits to be given to Rich Iannone and his `DiagrammeR` package.

Generally speaking, this package leverages HTML widgets to let you build an R diagram of nearly every kind.

Even if more advanced and customizable tools are available as standalone software, DiagrammeR lets you easily integrate different parts of your analysis without leaving R.

Moreover, DiagrammeR is perfectly integrated in RStudio and the **Shiny** framework, which is one among the hottest tools in R community.

Getting ready

As usual, we first have to install and load the necessary package, that is to say the `DiagrammeR` package:

```
install.packages("DiagrammeR")
library(DiagrammeR)
```

We are now ready to create a data frame that stores nodes and hedges of our process workflow.

Particularly, we will build an example from the healthcare environment regarding drugs administration.

How to do it...

1. We will start by creating a `nodes` data frame running `create_nodes()`.

   First of all, we need to create a data frame storing all process flow nodes, that is to say all steps composing the process we are looking at. This is done using `create_nodes()` and by passing ID, label, shape, and colors:

   ```
   nodes <- create_nodes(nodes = seq(1:7),
     label = c("select drug", "is it in stock?", "administer
     it",
     "adquire it","has it solved disease?",
     "look for another drug","end of treatment"),
     distortion = c(0,2,3,30),
     sides = 4,
     shape =  "rectangle",
     style = "filled",
     fillcolor = c("yellow", "lightgreen","azure",

     "azure","lightgreen","azure", "yellow")
   )
   ```

2. Next, we create a list of all connections. The second element of every kind of network, and process flows can be considered pertaining to this family as well, is a list of all connection linking nodes.

   To obtain this list, we will create the following `list` object composed of pairs of nodes IDs:

   ```
   edges_couples <-
   list(c(1,2),c(2,3),c(2,4),c(4,3),c(3,5),c(5,6),c(5,7),
   c(6,1))
   ```

3. We will now map the list to a from and to vector. In order to create diagram edges, we will call the `create_edges()` function that requires you to pass a from and a to vector. We will therefore export all first elements of our edge couple to the from vector and all second elements to the to vector:

```
from_vect <- c()
to_vect    <- c()
for(i in 1:length(edges_couples)) {
   from_vect <- c(from_vect,edges_couples[[i]][1])
   to_vect   <- c(to_vect,edges_couples[[i]][2])
}
```

4. We can now call the `create_edges()` function, passing the previously created from and to vectors, adding labels that we want to be shown on the edges:

```
edges <- create_edges(from = from_vect,
   to   = to_vect,
   label = c("","yes","no","","","no","yes"))
```

5. In this step, we will display the process flow diagram in RStudio Viewer.

   This step requires you to actually create a `graph` object through the `create_graph()` function and render it through `render_graph()`:

```
process_flow <- create_graph(nodes,edges,
   node_attrs = c("fontname = Helvetica
   color = grey80"),
   edge_attrs = c("color = lightblue",
   "arrowsize = 0.5"))
render_graph(process_flow)
```

   This will result in the following diagram appearing in your RStudio Viewer pane:

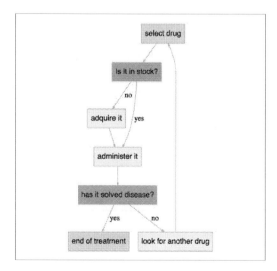

6. We can now export our diagram by leveraging the export control in the Viewer pane:

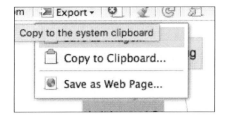

After clicking on **Copy to Clipboard**, the following window will appear, giving you the possibility to resize your picture before actually copying it to your clipboard:

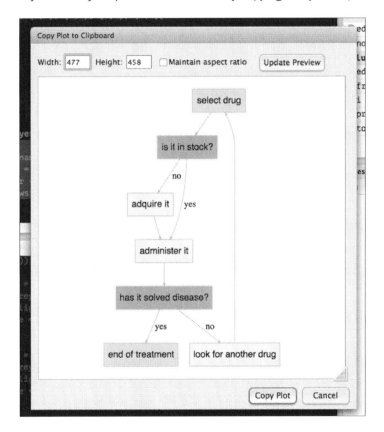

Once you are done with the resizing, you will just have to hit the **Copy Plot** button and paste your diagram where it is needed.

5
Power Programming with R

In this chapter, we will cover the following recipes:

- ▶ Writing modular code in RStudio
- ▶ Implementing parallel computation in R
- ▶ Creating custom objects and methods in R using the S3 system
- ▶ Evaluating your code performance using the `profvis` package
- ▶ Comparing an alternative function's performance using the `microbenchmarking` package
- ▶ Using GitHub with RStudio

Introduction

This chapter introduces you to a few advanced programming techniques in R, leveraging some of the unique features of the RStudio IDE, such as the embedded Git pane (refer to the last recipe of this chapter, *Using GitHub with RStudio*, to know more).

The recipes accomplished in this chapter are usually encountered by R programmers when dealing with large datasets (refer to the *Implementing parallel computation in R* recipe) and optimization issues (refer to the recipes on the `profvis` and `microbenchmarking` packages).

Writing modular code in RStudio

Using modular code is a best practice of computer programming. It basically involves dividing your code into independent pieces, where one module takes as an input the output of another one.

This recipe implements modular programming by leveraging the + function, which lets you execute R scripts from another script (or from the R terminal session itself) by collecting it in the local environment code output.

The advantage of modular code lies in the orthogonality principle: two pieces of code are orthogonal to each other if changing the first has no effect on the other.

Take, for instance, two pieces of code: the first one gives as an output a ZIP code from an address, and the second one takes that ZIP code and calculates the shipping cost for that ZIP code.

Until the first module gives a ZIP code as an output, the second module is totally unaware of how this code was defined. That is to say that any change in the first code will have no effect on the second one.

The Pragmatic Programmer by Andrew Hunt and David Thomas effectively shows this concept with the following graph:

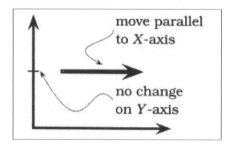

This diagram clearly exposes the concept: any movement parallel to the x axis will make no difference on the y axis, since they are orthogonal to each other.

Getting ready

In order to get our work done, we are going to first analyze the process we are going to model with a simple workflow diagram. We are going to draw the diagram, leveraging the DiagrammeR package by Rich Iannone:

```
install.packages("DiagrammeR")
library(DiagrammeR)
```

How to do it...

1. The first step is to define code workflow, outlying the input and output for each activity of the process.

    Refer to the recipe producing a process workflow diagram in RStudio in *Chapter 4, Advanced and Interactive Visualization* using the DiagrammeR package for workflow diagramming in R:

    ```
    node_attrs = c("fontname = Helvetica
      color = grey80"),
      edge_attrs = c("color = lightblue",
      "arrowsize = 0.5")
    define modules from your workflow
    ```

    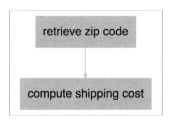

2. The next step is to define program scripts. In our example, we will have two modules:

    - ❏ `zip_retrievement`
    - ❏ `shipping_cost_retrievement`

    Write these two modules and place them in the current working directory in order to make them available for the following sourcing function:

    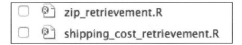

3. Next, we create a main script, sourcing the others. Our main script will basically source all the other scripts:

    ```
    source("zip_retrievement.R",local = TRUE)
    source("shipping_cost_retrievement.R", local = TRUE)
    ```

How it works...

In step 1 we define a workflow of your code, outlying the input and output for each activity of the process.

The first step is quite relevant, even if in our example it seems to be a simple one. In this step, we decide which activities performed from your code will be packed in one unique module.

You may ask, which rule could be used to decide which activities need to be put in a common module? Well, there is no scientific rule for this kind of choice; nevertheless, we can be led by two high-level principles, which are as follows:

  ▶ Clarity
  ▶ Ease of maintenance

Clarity will let us avoid over-decomposition of our code in hundreds of modules in order to preserve the overall readability of our code. Ease of maintenance will push us to join the pieces of code that will more realistically need maintenance at a common point in time.

That being said, we don't have to be too afraid of making mistakes, since this is an iterative process and we will always be able to perfect it.

In step 2, we write each module in a script. For the second step, the main point is addressing this question: couldn't we just create chunks of code in one unique R script?

Of course you could! Nevertheless, dividing your code into separate modules, both logically and physically, will let you gain a greater clarity about your code's logical flow.

Moreover, which is not to be underestimated, this will make you quickly understand if the orthogonality principle is respected in your code. This is because after changing something in a module, you will find an error coming up from another module, and you will then know that the two of them are not orthogonal to each other.

In step 3 we write a main script, sourcing the others. In the third step, the main script will do nothing more than source all modules in their logical sequence. The crucial point in this sourcing activity is the local argument that is set to `True`.

This argument tells R to store objects resulting from the sourced script in the general local environment. This act will make these objects available as input for the next sourced scripts.

Implementing parallel computation in R

Avoiding loops in R is a kind of good general principle (if you are not sure about that, take a look at this, a bit old but always great) post by Revolution Analytics at `http://blog.revolutionanalytics.com/2010/11/loops-in-r.html`.

The main reason why these kind of statements should be avoided is that R tends to handle your loops really slowly and, therefore, inefficiently.

Nevertheless, sometimes, these loops are really the only way to apply a given function or operation to your set of data. When dealing with these cases, and every time you are interested in improving your code efficiency, implementing parallel computation can give an important boost to your code.

The basic idea behind parallel computation is quite easy and described in the following points:

- Take the full job; you need to, for instance, calculate the square root of one thousand numbers in a vector
- Split it into smaller chunks of vector, *n*
- Send each chunk to one of the *n* workers that you previously created in your CPU cores
- Wait for the workers to do their job and send back results
- Combine the results in one object (going on with the example, we will have one thousand vectors storing the calculated squared roots)

Getting ready

On a Unix system, parallel computation can be implemented by leveraging the doParallel package, while on a Windows OS, you will rather use the doSNOW package:

```
install.packages("doParallel")
install.packages("doSNOW")
library(doParallel)
library(doSNOW)
```

How to do it...

1. The first step is to create workers (the maximum number is equal to the available core on your device or group of devices):

   ```
   cl = makeCluster(2)
   ```

2. Then, register the parallel session:

   ```
   registerDoParallel(cl) #unix OS
   registerDoSNOW(cl) #windows OS
   ```

3. After this, initialize the object that is to be worked on:

   ```
   vector <- seq(1:100000)
   ```

4. Apply your computation to the object with parallel computation:

```
result <- foreach(i = 1:length(vector), .combine= rbind)
%dopar% {
   return(vector[i]/sqrt(vector[i])^3)
}
```

5. Then, terminate the parallel session:

```
stopCluster(cl)
```

How it works...

In step one, we actually initialize two workers that are going to receive our job chunks and work on them.

You may think that's nice, but how many workers can I initialize? Infinite!

Unfortunately, this doesn't really make sense, since initializing a number of workers greater than your PC/PCs' cluster will not result in any improvement in efficiency.

The reason for this physical limit is that the core is the minimum unity that can perform an operation in your PC.

Therefore, the maximum number of workers will be equal to the number of available cores. To detect this number, you can leverage the detectCores() function from the parallel package:

```
install.packages(parallel)
parallel:detectCores()
```

If step one is a simple declaration of an object with no effect on your machine, running registerDoParallel will have the physical effect of initializing a parallel session. After performing step two, your workers will be waiting for their job.

In step four, we apply your computation on the object with parallel computation. The statement foreach() %dopar% {} is the actual piece of code that will take your complete job and separate it into smaller chunks, sending them to the workers you created.

The resulting objects received from the workers will be combined in a cumulative entity, following the value of the .combine argument:

▸ c: This will result in chunks being combined into a vector, which could also be applied in our example

▸ rbind and cbind: These will produce a matrix output

▸ +: This will add a numeric output into one resulting number

▸ *: This will multiply numeric outputs into one resulting number

There's more...

Given the increasing amount of data that is available and the consequent increasing average size of datasets we work with, parallel computation is quite a hot topic.

R provides a specific task view where you can learn about all the available tools and best practices for implementing this technique in R. You can find this task view at `https://cran.r-project.org/web/views/HighPerformanceComputing.html`.

Creating custom objects and methods in R using the S3 system

When dealing with a programming task pertaining to a specific business domain, developing custom objects with their related methods can enhance your work quality and usability.

Consider, for instance, a programmer dealing with a logistics project. Imagine him facing a choice of different types of means of transport packed with different attributes, cost functions, and time availability.

Defining different classes for these means of transport and adding proper attributes and methods to these classes will let you build a specific domain language that is able to represent, in a convenient way, the real problem you are trying to solve with your code. This concept is further explained in The Pragmatic Programmer by Andrew Hunt and David Thomas.

R comes packed with three different systems for object-oriented programming, which are as follows:

- The S3 system
- The S4 system
- Reference classes

In the following example, we are going to use the S3 system, define a custom truck class, add attributes, and a proper method to change the date of last maintenance.

How to do it...

1. The first step is to create the `truck` class with custom attributes:

```
trucks <- function(plate = "XXNNNZZ", night_trips = TRUE,
kilometers = 0, last_maintenance = "00/00/1900" ) {

  me <- structure(list(
    night_trips = night_trips,
    kilometers = kilometers,
```

```
        last_maintenance = last_maintenance
      ), class= "trucks")
    return(me)
  }
```

2. Next, we create a `volvo` truck specifying the plate, kilometers, and date of last maintenance:

```
volvo <- trucks(plate = "BE705WT",kilometers =
2000,last_maintenance = "17/01/2013")Add a method to set
maintenance date after first initialization
set_last_maintenance <- function(entity,value_to_set) {
  UseMethod("set_last_maintenance",entity)
}
set_last_maintenance.default <-
function(entity,value_to_set) {
  return(NULL)
}
set_last_maintenance.trucks <-
function(entity,value_to_set) {
  entity$last_maintenance <- value_to_set
  message("maintenance date was set correctly")
  return(entity)
}
```

3. Then, we change the maintenance date:

```
volvo <- set_last_maintenance(volvo,"10/01/2016")Check
results
volvo$last_maintenance
```

How it works...

In step 1, we create the `truck` class with custom attributes. In the first step, new classes are declared with a function-like syntax, where the default values for class attributes are passed as arguments. In the body of the function, an inner reference is made using the pronoun `me` in order to refer to the function itself.

Using this terminology, the class attributes and names are declared. Finally, with the `return(me)` statement, the new `truck` class is returned as a value for the function.

At the end of this procedure, a new `trucks` function will be stored in your environment, as made clear by the RStudio environment explorer:

```
Functions
    set_last_maintena... function (entity, value_to_set)
    set_last_maintena... function (entity, value_to_set)
    trucks              function (plate = "XXNNNZZ", night_trips = TRUE...
```

In step 2, we create a Volvo truck, specifying the plate, kilometers, and date of last maintenance. This step simply involves calling the `trucks()` function and assigning a function value to the `volvo` object.

Once again, the RStudio environment explorer clearly shows the class attribute for the newly arrived `volvo` entity:

```
volvo           List of 3
    night_trips : logi TRUE
    kilometers : num 2000
    last_maintenance: chr "17/01/2013"
    attr(*, "class")= chr "trucks"
```

In step 3 we add a method to set a maintenance date after first initialization. The third step basically involves three activities, which are as follows:

▶ Defining a generic `set_last_maintenance` function.

▶ Defining a value to be returned in case the function is called on an object which is not of class `truck`.

▶ Defining a function's resulting value when dealing with an object of the `trucks` class. In this last step, we tell the function what to do with the trucks object being passed to it.

Particularly, with the `entity$last_maintenance <- value_to_set` statement, we tell the function to change the `last_maintenance` attribute to a value that was passed to the function.

The final statement `return(entity)` is very important. The lack of this causes the changes made in this function to have no effect on the outside environment.

Evaluating your code performance using the profvis package

The profvis package is a powerful tool for line profiling in R.

This package is provided by the RStudio team, and its most appreciated feature is the interactive report that is automatically produced, representing a really effective way of visualizing and investigating time resources requested by each part of your code.

Getting ready

Since the lineprof package is not hosted on CRAN, but on GitHub, we first need it to install the devtools package in order to leverage the install_github function provided by this package.

Moreover, we will use the ggmap package to build the example to be profiled:

```
install.packages(c("devtools","ggmap"))
library(devtools)
install_github("rstudio/profvis")
library(profvis)
library(ggmap)
```

How to do it...

1. Define a profvis object containing the code to be profiled. Run the following piece of code, initializing the report object.

2. The following code is used from the drawing a route on a map with ggmap recipe in *Chapter 3, Basic Visualization Techniques*; refer to the recipe for further details:

```
report <- profvis ({
  library(ggmap)
  trip <- (route(from = "rome", to = "milan",structure =
  "route", output = "simple"))
  segment <- c()
  for(i in 1:nrow(trip)) {
    if(i == 1){segment[i] <- 1}else {
      if( i %% 2 != 0 ) {
        segment [i] <- i-segment[i-1]}else {
          segment [i] <- i/2
        }
      }
    }
}
```

```
segment_couple <- c(0,segment[-length(segment)])


trip$segment <- segment
trip$segment_couple <- segment_couple
route_map <- get_map("italy",zoom = 6)
ggmap(route_map) +
  geom_point(aes(x = lon, y = lat, size = 5, colour =
  hours),data = trip) +
  geom_line(data = trip,aes(group = segment)) +
  geom_line(data = trip, aes(group = segment_couple))


})Print the object runing print(report)
```

This will open a web browser window, showing an interactive profiling report similar to the following:

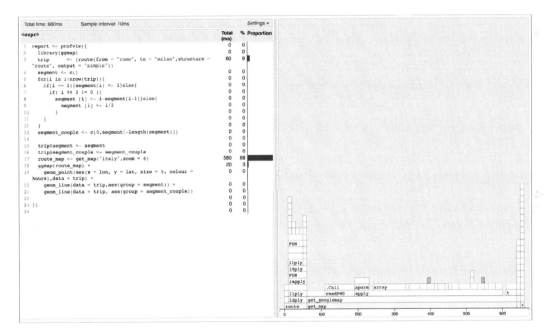

In the preceding screenshot, on the left-hand side, you can find your code produced line by line, where each line has, on the right-hand side, a count of the required milliseconds for running and a count of the proportion of the time on the total running time. On the right-hand side part of the report, a *barchart-like* interactive plot is produced, where the bottom line represents the first function that was called and the upper bars represent the functions called by those first functions. You can hide lines of code having zero running time. On the top-right corner of the left-hand side part of your report, you can find a **Settings** control. Selecting it will open the following menu:

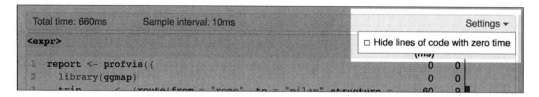

Selecting the checkbox next to **Hide lines of code with zero time** will result in hiding of all the lines of code that have a running time less than a millisecond:

<expr>	Total (ms)	% Proportion	
3 trip <- {route(from = "rome", to = "milan",structure = "route", output = "simple")}	60	9	
17 route_map <- get_map("italy",zoom = 6)	580	88	
18 ggmap(route_map) +	20	3	

3. Focus on a single line of code. Selecting a single piece of plot on the right-hand side of the window will let you zoom in on that piece and all the bars that come from that first bar. Save the report as a web page (use the *cmd* + S or *Ctrl* + S shortcut).

Running *cmd* + S on Mac devices, or *Ctrl* + S on Windows devices, will let you save your report as a fully functional web page:

report.html

Comparing an alternative function's performance using the microbenchmarking package

When dealing with efficiency issues, a fast way to evaluate two alternative functions can be really useful.

This recipe is going to show you how to do this quickly and effectively and display the results of your comparison in a `ggplot` diagram that is easy to understand.

Getting ready

This recipe is going to leverage the `microbenchmark` package to compute the function comparison and the `ggplot2` package for comparison plotting:

```
install.packages(c("microbenchmark","ggplot2"))
library(microbenchmark)
library(ggplot2)
```

The example that follows is represented by two alternative functions to determine, for a given numeric vector, which elements of the vector are even and which are odd.

Therefore, we first need to initialize the vector we are going to use, populating it with a sequence of numbers from 1 to 1000:

```
vector <- seq(1:1000)
```

How to do it...

1. First, we need to define the functions that are to be compared. In order to test code efficiency, you need to expose your pieces of code into a functional shape. The following is an example involving the `ifelse()` vectorized function and the standard `if()else{}` statement:

```
vectorised_if <- function(vector) {
  result <- c()
  for(i in 1:length(vector)) {
  ifelse(vector[i]%%2==0,result[i] <- "even",result[i] <-
  "odd")
  }
  return(result)
}
standard_if <- function(vector) {
  result <- c()
```

```
      for(i in 1:length(vector)) {
        if(vector[i]%%2 ==0){ result[i] <- "even"}
        else{result[i] <- "odd"}
      }
      return(result)
  }
```

2. Create a `microbenckmark` object by passing the two functions that we defined
    previously to the `microbenchmark()` function:

    ```
    comparison <- microbenchmark(standard_if(vector),
    vectorised_if(vector), times = 100)
    ```

    What the `microbenchmark()` function does is run the two (or more) functions
    a number *n* of times (specified from the times argument), recording running
    time. This lets you understand which function requires less time to run. Plot the
    `microbenchmark` object.

    The `microbenchmark` objects can be easily plotted using a built-in `autoplot()`
    function, as follows:

    ```
    autoplot(comparison)
    ```

    Calling this function on a `comparison` object will result in the viewer pane showing
    up the following plot:

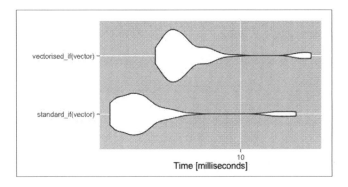

For each one of the two functions, a frequency distribution of the times it's run is shown,
assuming this typical mandolin shape. In our example, quite surprisingly, the `standard_`
`if()` function shows consistently better performance. For more information, refer to
the comparison details. A summary function is provided to gain greater insights on the
performed simulations and results:

```
  summary(comparison)
                      expr         min         lq       mean     median
   uq         max neval
```

```
1    standard_if(vector) 3.354620 3.732035 4.540858 4.157452
4.524025 16.54318    100
2 vectorised_if(vector) 4.987396 5.497869 7.387133 6.009339
6.891614 19.61941    100
```

This summary shows the min, max, mean, median, and lower and upper quartile, for each evaluated function.

Using GitHub with RStudio

Have you ever found yourself looking desperately at your RStudio console showing a runtime error? Doesn't it make you think of those wonderful moments a few days ago, where you were happily executing your code?

Have you ever thought "If I just had a time machine, I would go back to those days!"?

Well, what we will show you here is exactly that—a way to add your RStudio project to a time machine.

The name of this time machine is Git, which is a popular version-control system created by Linus Torvald; yes, he is the same guy who created Linux.

The basic rationale behind this kind of software is quite simple: the changes within a script (and actually every kind of file) are stored in commits and all commits are stored in one repository.

In every moment of code development is possible to restore previous commits and get back in time.

Git actually offers a lot more, for example, letting you create branches in your code, to develop and test new features or just fix bugs, and then merge them back into main repository, integrating only the differences.

The place where these commits are stored in an ordered way is called a **repository**. There are several web services for online repository hosting, but the most popular one is **GitHub**. This platform has been around since 2008, and can now boast about hosting websites by Google, Microsoft, and other prestigious software companies.

Getting ready

First of all, you need to install Git on your device. You can find the appropriate version of your software at `http://git-scm.com/downloads`.

After downloading and installing Git, you are now ready to link it with RStudio and start using it on an RStudio project.

How to do it...

1. The first step is to link Git with RStudio. To apply this step, you first need to locate your `git.exe` file (on PC) or `git.app` on Mac. You can do this from RStudio's **Global Options...**:

Once the **Global Options...** window is open, you will need to place the path on your Git application in the **Git executable** field, as shown in the following screenshot:

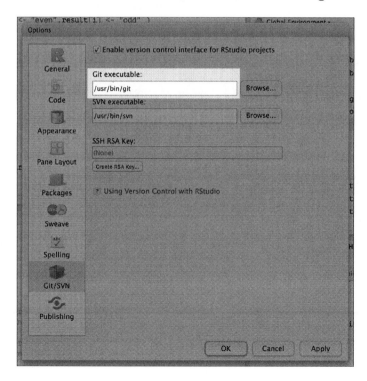

2. The next step is to launch **Shell**. You can easily find the **Shell...** control under the **Tools** menu:

3. Now we need to authenticate to Git. In the just-launched shell, write your GitHub username and e-mail ID:

```
git config --global user.name "AndreaCirilloAC"
git config --global user.email "andreacirilloac@gmail.com"
```

4. Create a new repository on GitHub from www.github.com:

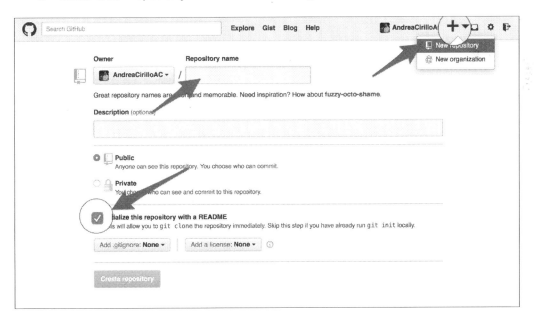

5. Copy the repository's SSH address. You can find the SSH address directly in the window that you will access after creating the repository:

6. Create a new RStudio project. After selecting the new project control, select the version control option:

Then, select the **Git** option:

7. Paste the copied SSH address, as shown in the following figure:

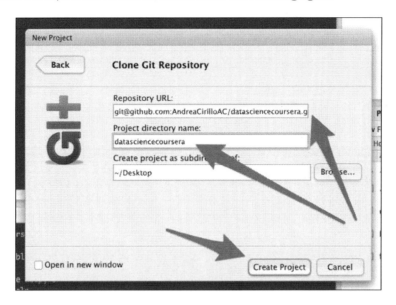

8. Submit your first commit. Just to be sure that everything is OK, you can commit whatever you like in your GitHub repository.

   This can be done in the **Git** tab on the upper-right side of the toolbar of your RStudio window, as shown in the following screenshot:

   After making changes to your R script (or any other file within your repository), you will be able to commit it using the **Commit** control visible in the preceding screenshot.

To commit something, you first need to check the corresponding file in the list associated with the **Git** pane:

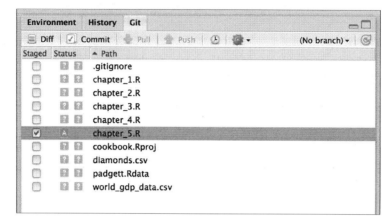

Clicking on the **Commit** control on the upper-left side of the **Git** tab will then result in the following new window:

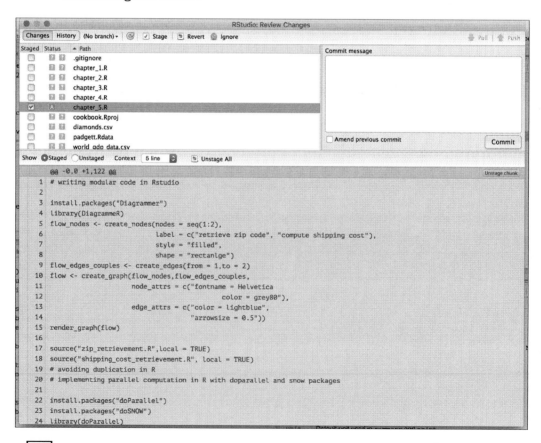

In this window, you will be able to see all the changes made to your code from the previous commit (green highlights are used for code addition, while red highlights are reserved for deletion). Every commit will need to be associated with a commit message.

Clicking on the **Commit** button will result in a pop-up window and confirm the successful end of the committing step:

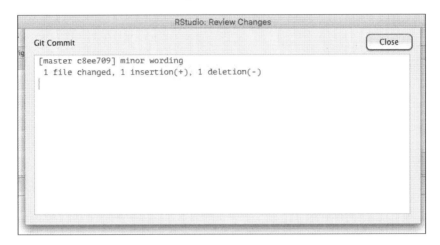

9. Go back to the GitHub repository. After performing a reasonable number of commits (this is just common sense, since no minimum level is required), you can now send your commits to the online GitHub repository, by clicking the **Push** button:

A new window will pop up, and a message will confirm the successful end of your push to the GitHub server:

10. Next, visualize your commits history. As promised at the beginning of this chapter, we are going to see the full history of your code here by just clicking on the clock placed in the **Git** tab of RStudio:

This will pop up a new window, showing all the performed commits. As usual, you will find that highlighted in red lines deleted with that given commit, and green-colored added lines of code:

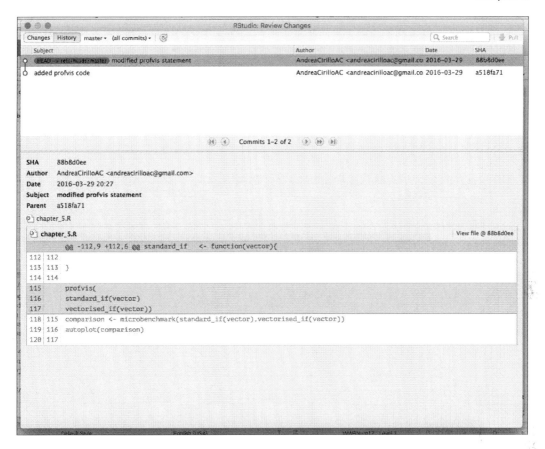

This is great, isn't it? If you are already falling in love with the Git version control system, you just have to look at the next section to know where to look for further information on your new-found love.

There's more...

As you are already guessing, Git is a really powerful tool for programming tasks, particularly when working in a team.

Describing the advantages and the complete list of functionalities of Git is out of the scope of this recipe; nevertheless, I would like to point out a really good introductory interactive tutorial on Git provided by **Code School**, which can be found at `https://try.github.io`.

If you are looking for something more articulate and complete, you can always turn to the official project website, `http://git-scm.com/`.

6
Domain-specific Applications

In this chapter, we will cover the following topics:

- ▶ Dealing with regular expressions
- ▶ Analyzing PDF reports in a folder with the `tm` package
- ▶ Creating wordclouds with the `wordcloud` package
- ▶ Performing a Twitter sentiment analysis
- ▶ Detecting fraud in e-commerce orders with Benford's law
- ▶ Measuring customer retention using cohort analysis in R
- ▶ Making a recommendation engine
- ▶ Performing time series decomposition using the `stl()` function
- ▶ Exploring time series forecasting with `forecast()`
- ▶ Tracking stock movements using the `quantmode` package
- ▶ Optimizing portfolio composition and maximizing returns with the Portfolio Analytics package
- ▶ Forecasting the stock market

Introduction

I have to be honest: one of the things I love the most about R is the huge amount of domain-specific packages.

I am sure you know that feeling. You start working on a new topic, let's say financial portfolio optimization. You start studying a bit of theory and then ask yourself, "Will there be an R package for this?"

In 90 percent cases, the answer will be "Yes." Actually, if R can be considered a powerful programming language, it is in domain-specific applications that we can appreciate its true power.

As of June 24, 2015, 6,712 packages for Windows OS were computed. We could even paraphrase that well-known Apple remark into:

> *"There's a package for that."*

Chapter 7, Developing Static Reports, which follows, highlights this R richness, showing 13 domain applications where specific packages play a central role.

Dealing with regular expressions

Regular expressions let you easily perform string manipulation with the help of just a handful of characters. In this recipe, we will look for digits, punctuation, and uppercase and lowercase in a vector of strings.

How to do it...

1. Define a `test` vector that you can search with regular expressions:

   ```
   test_string <- c("012","345",";.","kdj","KSR" ,"\n")
   ```

2. Look for digits:

   ```
   grep("[[:digit:]]",test_string, value = TRUE)
   which will result in :
   [1] "012" "345"
   ```

3. Look for punctuation:

   ```
   grep("[[:punct:]]",test_string, value = TRUE)
   which will have as a result
   [1] ";."
   ```

4. Look for lowercase letters:

```
grep("[[:lower:]]",test_string, value = TRUE)
```

Which will select the following:

```
[1] "kdj"
```

5. Look for uppercase letters:

```
grep("[[:upper:]]",test_string, value = TRUE)
```

Which will select only upper cases:

```
[1] "KSR"
```

Analyzing PDF reports in a folder with the tm package

Text analytics is basically a way to perform quantitative analysis on qualitative information stored in text. In this recipe, we will create a corpus of documents from PDF files and perform descriptive analytics on them, looking for the most frequent terms.

This is a particularly useful recipe for professionals who work with PDF reports.

In this recipe, we will explore the full text of the Italian medieval masterpiece *Divine Comedy* by Dante Alighieri. You can find out more on Wikipedia at `https://en.wikipedia.org/wiki/Divine_Comedy`:

Source: `http://www.theimaginativeconservative.org/category/great-books/dante`

Dante Alighieri is shown holding a copy of the `Divine Comedy`, next to the entrance to Hell, the seven terraces of Mount Purgatory and the city of Florence, with the spheres of Heaven above, in Michelino's fresco.

Getting ready

In this recipe, we will use the `pdftotext` utility in order to read text from the PDF format.

You can download `pdftotext` from `http://www.foolabs.com/xpdf/download.html`. Depending on the operating system you are working on, you will have to perform different steps in order to properly install the package. Proper instructions can be found in the `INSTALL` file that comes with each package.

Once you are done with `pdftotext`, it is time to install the required packages:

```
install.packages(c("tm","ggplot2","wordcloud"))
library(tm)
library(ggplot2)
library(wordcloud)
```

How to do it...

1. Define the directory where PDF reports are stored:

   ```
   directory <- c("pdf_files")
   ```

2. Create a `corpus` object from your reports:

   ```
   corpus <- Corpus(DirSource(directory),
     readerControl = list( reader = readPDF(), language =
     "it", encoding = "UTF-8"))
   ```

3. Remove punctuation:

   ```
   corpus <- tm_map(corpus,removePunctuation)
   ```

4. Remove numbers:

   ```
   corpus <- tm_map(corpus,removeNumbers)
   ```

5. Change capital letters to lowercase:

   ```
   corpus <- tm_map(corpus,tolower)
   ```

6. Remove stop words:

   ```
   corpus <- tm_map(corpus,removeWords,stopwords(kind = "it"))
   ```

7. Put every document into plain text format:

```
corpus <- tm_map(corpus,PlainTextDocument)
```

8. Define a document term matrix:

```
term_matrix <- DocumentTermMatrix(corpus)
```

9. Remove infrequent terms (sparse terms):

```
term_matrix <- removeSparseTerms(term_matrix,0.2)
```

10. Find out the most frequents words:

```
frequent_words <- (colSums(as.matrix(term_matrix)))
frequent_words <- as.data.frame(frequent_words)
frequent_words <- data.frame(
(row.names(frequent_words)),frequent_words)
colnames(frequent_words) <- c("term","frequency")
frequent_words$terms <- levels(frequent_words$terms)
row.names(frequent_words) <- c()
```

11. Remove insignificant terms:

```
to_be_removed <-
c("mai","<e8>","<ab>","s<ec>","pi<f9>","<f2>",
   "<ab>cos<ec>","<e0>","<e0>","s<e9>","perch<e9>",
   "gi<f9>","f<e9>","ch<e8>","cos<ec>","gi<e0>","tanto","
   ch<e9>",  "n<e9>")
indexes <- match(to_be_removed,frequent_words$term)
frequent_words <- frequent_words[-indexes,]
```

12. Filter for only frequent terms:

```
frequent_words <- frequent_words[frequent_words$frequency >
100,]
```

13. Plot your frequent works:

```
plot <- ggplot(frequent_words, aes(term, frequency)) +
geom_bar(stat = "identity") +
theme(axis.text.x = element_text(angle = 45, hjust=1))
plot
```

Let's take a look at the following graph:

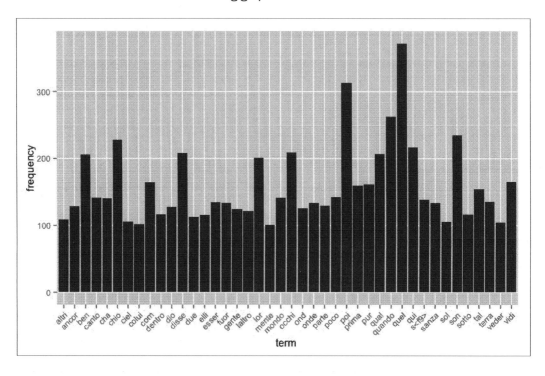

How it works...

In step 1, we define the directory where pdf reports are stored. Our first step set the path to the directory to store all PDF reports to be read.

Be aware that since we are performing this analysis within the RStudio project related to this book, the working directory is automatically set to the directory where the project is executed from. We just need to specify the name of the relative path of the folder, that is, the part of path from the working directory to the required folder.

In step 2, we create a `corpus` object from your reports. Corpora are the basic objects for text analytics analysis. A corpus can be considered a collection of documents you are going to analyze. We initialized a `corpus` object, adding to it all documents within the directory specified in the previous step.

Arguments of the `Corpus()` function are:

- ▶ Directory path
- ▶ Reader to be used for document loading; this is where the previously installed `pdftotext` comes to hand

- ▶ Document language
- ▶ Character encoding (UTF-8 in our case)

In step 3 to 6, we prepare corpus for analysis. Preparing our corpus for analysis involves the following activities:

- ▶ Removing punctuation, which gives no added value to our analysis but can modify counts and stats on the corpus content
- ▶ Removing numbers, for a similar reason to punctuation
- ▶ Transforming all capital letters to lowercase so that the same words with and without capital letters are not counted twice
- ▶ Removing stop words, such as "not," "or," or "and;" stop words can also be customized by passing a custom defined vector of stop words to the `tm_map()` function

After performing those activities, our corpus will be ready for our analysis.

In step 8, we define a document term `matrixDocument`; term matrixes are matrixes representing the frequency of terms that occur in a corpus. Within a document term matrix, rows correspond to documents in the collection, and columns represent terms.

We define a document term matrix by running the `DocumentTermMatrix()` function on our `corpus` object.

In step 9, we remove infrequent terms. In this step, we define a minimum frequency threshold under which we consider words to not interest us. Be aware that sparsity is defined as a percentage, in which:

- ▶ 0 is the bigger sparsity represented by words that do not appear within the corpus
- ▶ 1 is the smaller sparsity, that is, words with the maximum observed frequency

In step 10, we find out the most frequent words. This step computes the total frequency for each word on the all corpus using the `colSums()` function. It then creates a data frame composed of terms and frequency.

In step 11, we remove meaningless terms. This step is specifically related to PDF documents since it results in removing the reading error in order to prevent errors within the final stat. For instance, we remove `<e8>`, which is a wrong reading of the character è, which stand for "is" in Italian.

In step 12, we remove infrequent words, leveraging the previously computed term frequencies and setting a threshold at 100 repetitions.

In step 13, we now plot our data, leveraging a basic `ggplot` package. Refer to the *Adding text to a ggplot2 plot at a custom location* recipe in *Chapter 3, Basic Visualization Techniques,* which provides a good introduction to these plots.

Creating word clouds with the wordcloud package

Word clouds are a nice and useful way to show text composition at a glance.

In a word cloud, words composing a text are composed in a kind of cloud, and usually their size and color is related to the frequency of the given term in the source text.

In this way, it is possible to understand quickly which words are more relevant to the given text. In this recipe, we will explore the Wikipedia page related to the R programming language.

Getting ready

We first need to install the required packages and load them into the R environment:

```
install.packages(c("wordcloud","RColorBrewer","rvest"))
library(wordcloud)
library(rvest)
library(RColorBrewer)
```

How to do it...

1. Define your document URL and download it in the R environment:

    ```
    url <-
    "https://en.wikipedia.org/wiki/R_(programming_language)"
    page <- read_html(url)
    page <- html_text(page,trim = TRUE)
    page <- gsub("\n","",page, fixed = FALSE)
    page <- gsub("\t","",page, fixed = FALSE)
    ```

2. Print out your word cloud:

    ```
    wordcloud(page)
    ```

3. Filter for most frequent terms:

    ```
    wordcloud(page,min.freq = 4)
    ```

4. Change the color combination of words:

    ```
    palette <- brewer.pal(n = 9, "Paired")
    wordcloud(page,colors = palette)
    ```

Let's take a look at the following image:

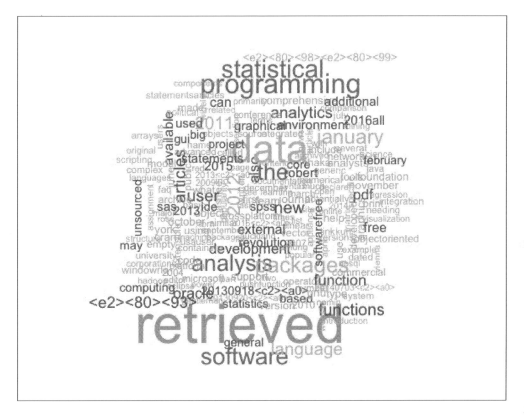

How it works...

Our first step involves storing the Wikipedia page URL in an on-purpose variable and downloading the HTML code stored on that page.

HTML reading is done through the `read_html()` function from the `rvest` package.

After performing this step, we downloaded all the HTML code, including the HTML tags such as `<h1>` and `<a href>`.

In order to remove these tags and focus on the proper text, we just have to run `html_text()` on the created `page` object.

We then remove `\t` and `\n`, since they are just escaping characters.

In step 2, we print out our word cloud. Creating our word cloud is as easy as running the `wordcloud()` function on the `page` object.

Be aware that some default argument values apply here:

> ▸ The size of each word in the cloud is proportional to the frequency of the word within the `text` object. If not specified, the frequency argument would be automatically computed within the function.

> ▸ The `min.freq` argument is set to 3 by default, meaning that words that appear less than three times will not show up within your word cloud.

In step 3, we filter for the most frequent terms. As said earlier, the frequency filter is set through the `min.freq` parameter. Changing the parameter will consequently lead to changes in the number of words displayed.

In step 4, we change the words' color combinations. By leveraging `Rcolorbrewer`, we can easily define palettes of colors to use to color our word cloud.

To look at the available palettes, just run the following command on your R console:

```
display.brewer.all()
```

This function will produce the following plot:

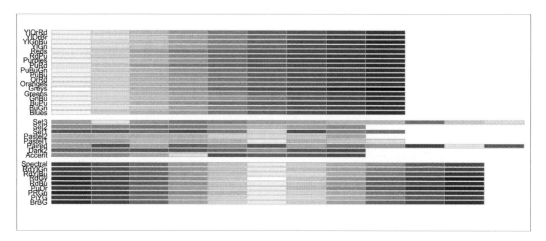

Labels placed on the left-hand side of the plot can be substituted to be "paired" within `palette <- brewer.pal(n = 9, "Paired")`.

That said, you should be aware that changing the *n* argument will change the number of colors retrieved from the given brewer palette for your custom palette.

Performing a Twitter sentiment analysis

Twitter sentiment analysis is another powerful tool in the text analytics toolbox.

With sentiment analysis, we can analyze the mood expressed within a text.

In this recipe, we will download tweets relating to "data science with R" and perform a sentiment analysis on them, employing the bag of word technique.

The main feature of this technique is not trying to understand the meaning of the analyzed text but just looking at one word at the time, seeing whether it expresses a positive or negative sentiment.

Our example will therefore result in computing the overall sentiment around the topic, algebraically summing up the sentiment score of every single word in our bag.

Getting ready

This recipe will leverage powerful functions from three different packages: one for downloading tweets, one for string manipulation, and the last one for text analytics activities.

We therefore need to install and load those packages:

```
install.packages(c("twitteR","stringr","tm"))
library(twitteR)
library(stringr)
library(tm)
```

How to do it...

1. Set up a Twitter session.

   Refer to *Chapter 1, Acquiring Data for Your Project*, and the *Getting data from Twitter with the twitteR package* recipe for further details on how to set up a Twitter application:

   ```
   setup_twitter_oauth(consumer_key    = 'xxxx',
     consumer_secret = 'xxxx',
     access_token    = 'xxxx',
     access_secret   = 'xxxx')
   ```

2. Download tweets pertaining to a specific query:

   ```
   tweet_list <- searchTwitter('"data science with R"', n = 20)
   ```

3. Create a data frame with the downloaded tweets:

```
tweet_df    <-  twListToDF(tweet_list)
```

4. Define positive and negative words:

```
pos_words = read.csv("lexicon/positive.txt",header =
FALSE,stringsAsFactors=FALSE)

pos_words <- c(pos_words)

pos_words <- unlist(pos_words)

pos_words <- unname(pos_words)

pos_words <- tolower(pos_words)

neg_words = read.csv("lexicon/negative.txt",header =
FALSE,stringsAsFactors=FALSE)

neg_words <- c(neg_words)

neg_words <- unlist(neg_words)

neg_words <- unname(neg_words)

neg_words <- tolower(neg_words)
```

5. Extract tweet text from the tweets database:

```
tweets <- tweet_df[,1]
```

6. Clean up tweets with the gsub() function and a regular expression:

```
tweets <- gsub('[[:punct:]]', '', tweets)

tweets <- gsub('[[:cntrl:]]', '', tweets)

tweets <- gsub('\\d+', '', tweets)

tweets <- gsub("RT", '',tweets)

tweets <- gsub("⊠», <>,tweets)
```

7. Remove stopwords:

```
tweets <- removeWords(tweets,stopwords(kind = "en"))
```

8. Split tweets into words using str_split() function from stringr package: *n = 140*, maximum number of letters:

```
word_df    <- str_split_fixed(tweets, '\\s+',n = 140)

word_df    <- data.frame(word_df,"RT" = tweet_df[,12])

word_count <- melt(word_df,id <- c("RT"))

word_df    <- data.frame( "word" = word_count[,3],
  "RT" = word_count[,1])
```

9. Match each word with its lexicon:

```
word_df$is_positive <- match(unlist(word_count[,3]),
pos_words)

word_df$is_negative <-
match(unlist(word_count[,3]),neg_words)
```

10. Remove blank rows:

```
word_df <- subset(word_df,word_df[,1] != "")
```

11. Define the scoring function:

```
sentiment_scorer  <- function(pos_match,neg_match) {
  if (is.na(pos_match) && is.na(neg_match)) {0}
  else {
    if(is.na(pos_match) && is.na(neg_match) == FALSE){-
1} else
    {1}
  }


}
```

12. Apply the `sentiment_scorer()` function:

```
word_df <- data.frame(word_df,score =
mapply(sentiment_scorer,word_df$is_positive,
word_df$is_negative))
```

13. Compute a final score by multiplying the score by the number of retweets:

```
popularity_scorer <- function(rt,basic_score) {
  if(rt == 0){basic_score}
  else{rt * basic_score}
}


word_df$final_score <-
mapply(popularity_scorer,word_df$RT,word_df$score)
```

14. Show the results:

```
total_df <-
aggregate(word_df$final_score,list(word_df$word),sum)

cloud     <- wordcloud(total_df$Group,abs(total_df$x),
scale=c(10,.20),colors=brewer.pal(10,"Spectral"))
```

Find out the total sentiment score:

```
total_sentiment <- sum(word_df$final_score)
```

How it works...

In step 3, we define positive and negative words. This step involves reading the `positive.txt` and `negative.txt` files in the R environment and manipulating them in order to produce a familiar vector, such as the following one:

```
> head(pos_words)
[1] "a+"         "abound"      "abounds"     "abundance"   "abundant"
"accessable"
```

Since we read our words from a txt file and the contents first come into R as a list, we first have to unlist the `pos_words` list and remove the row names.

A final touch is added, changing all capital letters to lowercase in order to ensure comparability with tweet text.

In step 5, we clean up tweets with `gsub()` and regular expressions. In this step, we remove punctuation and other specific words from our tweets, iterating the `gsub()` application on them.

This function only requires that you have a pattern to look for and an object that you can look for the pattern.

In step 6, we remove stopwords. Stopwords are words such as "and", "or," "even," and other common words in a language. Since they add no great value to the text in terms of comprehension, they are usually removed.

If you want to have a look at those words, you just need to run the following command:

```
> head(stopwords(kind = "en"))
[1] "i"         "me"      "my"      "myself" "we"      "our"
```

In step 7, we split tweets into words. Using the `str_split_fixed()` function, we split our tweets into separate words in order to apply text analytics techniques on them, like the ones seen in the previous recipes.

This function requires that you specify two main arguments:

- ▶ The string to split
- ▶ The pattern to look for in order to define the splitting points

After applying this function to all our tweets, we now have a data frame with the following structure:

- ▶ First word; second word; third word
- ▶ First word; second word; NA; NA
- ▶ First word; NA; NA; NA

Here, each row corresponds to a tweet.

Since we will use the number of retweets in order to compute our final sentiment score, we will now add this information to the data frame with the following line of code:

```
word_df <- data.frame(word_df,"RT" = tweet_df[,12])
```

Once we do this, the data frame will look like this:

- First word; second word; third word; 20
- First word; second word; NA; NA; 14
- First word; NA; NA; NA; 2

This is not what we need yet, since our minimum object of analysis is the single word.

What we are looking for is actually a tidy dataset, like the ones introduced in *Chapter 2, Preparing for Analysis – Data Cleansing and Manipulation*, where each row stores an observation.

In order to obtain this kind of dataset, we will apply the `melt()` function, which will create a unique column from all words, replicating the number of retweets received from the tweet for each word.

In step 8, we match word with lexicon. In this step, we associate two new attributes to the `word_df` data frame:

- The `is_positive` data frame, which is true for words that are found within the `pos_words` vector of positive words.
- The `is_negative` data frame, which is true for words that are found within the `neg_words` vector.

We then removed words that are neither positive nor negative, and are therefore not relevant for sentiment analysis purposes.

In step 9, we define a scoring function. Our scoring function assigns 1 to every positive word and -1 to every negative word. Quite linear, isn't it?

In step 10, we apply the function. We now apply the defined function to our real data, obtaining a new `score` attribute, which applies 1 for positive words and -1 for negative words.

In step 11, we compute a final score by multiplying the score by the number of retweets. Since we want to take into consideration the number of retweets of a single tweet, we define a new function. In the case of the absence of retweets, this function leaves the score untouched, while where retweets are found, it will multiply the score by the number of retweets.

Applying this function over the vector of words and scores will result in a new column, named `final_score`, containing weighted scores.

You may be asking, "So, the sentiment of a tweet increases if it gets retweeted?"

Well, we are actually measuring the sentiment around a topic, not a single tweet sentiment (and the topic is the one defined in step 2).

We therefore count 1 for each positive tweet and -1 for each negative tweet.

If a tweet got retweeted, we consider it as another positive/negative tweet on that topic, therefore adding +1/-1.

This is actually a distinctive point of this analysis, since usually data mining activities around downloaded tweets make it impossible to take retweets into account.

In step 12, we show the results. This step performs two tasks:

- ▶ It creates a final data frame, `final_df`, where the sum of scores are obtained for each word (aggregating repeated words).

- ▶ It plots a word cloud where the size of each word is related to the absolute value of the final score of that word.

In step 13, we look at the total sentiment score. Since the score of positive words are positive numbers and score of negative words are negative numbers, we can sum up all scores and understand whether the general mood around the given search key is positive or negative.

Detecting fraud in e-commerce orders with Benford's law

Benford's law is a popular empirical law that states that the first digits of a population of data will follow a specific logarithmic distribution.

This law was observed by Frank Benford around 1938 and since then has gained increasing popularity as a way to detect anomalous alterations in a population of data.

Basically, testing a population against Benford's law means verifying that the given population respects this law. If deviations are discovered, the law performs further analysis for items related to those deviations.

In this recipe, we will test a population of e-commerce orders against the law, focusing on items deviating from the expected distribution.

Getting ready

This recipe will use functions from the well-documented `benford.analysis` package by Carlos Cinelli.

We therefore need to install and load this package:

```
install.packages("benford.analysis")
library(benford.analysis)
```

In our example, we will use a data frame that stores e-commerce orders, provided within the book as an `.Rdata` file.

In order to make it available within your environment, we need to load this file by running the following command (assuming the file is in your current working directory):

```
load("ecommerce_orders_list.Rdata")
```

How to do it...

1. Perform the Benford test on the order amounts:

   ```
   benford_test <-
   benford(ecommerce_orders_list$order_amount,1)
   ```

2. Plot the test analysis:

   ```
   plot(benford_test)
   ```

   This will result in the following plot:

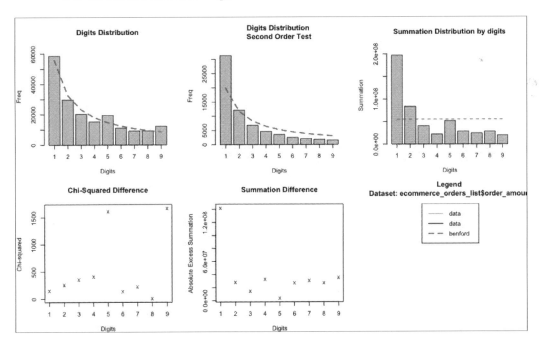

3. Highlight digits deviating from expected distribution:

```
suspectsTable(benford_test)
```

This will produce a table showing, for each digit, the absolute differences between expected and observed frequencies. The first digits will therefore be the anomalous ones:

```
> suspectsTable(benford_test)
   digits absolute.diff
1:      5      4860.8974
2:      9      3764.0664
3:      1      2876.4653
4:      2      2870.4985
5:      3      2856.0362
6:      4      2706.3959
7:      7      1567.3235
8:      6      1300.7127
9:      8       200.4623
```

4. Define a function to extrapolate the first digit from each amount:

```
left = function (string,char) {
    substr(string,1,char)}
```

5. Extrapolate the first digit from each amount:

```
ecommerce_orders_list$first_digit <-
left(ecommerce_orders_list$order_amount,1)
```

6. Filter amounts starting with the suspected digit:

```
suspects_orders <- subset(ecommerce_orders_list,first_digit
== 5)
```

How it works...

In step 1, we perform the Benford test on the order amounts. In this step, we apply the `benford()` function to the amounts.

Applying this function means evaluating the distribution of the first digits of amounts against the expected Benford distribution.

The function will result in the production of the following objects:

Info	General information, including: ▶ `data.name`: The name of the data used ▶ `n`: The number of observations used ▶ `n.second.order`: The number of observations used for second-order analysis ▶ `number.of.digits`: The number of first digits analyzed
Data	A data frame with: ▶ `lines.used`: The original lines of the dataset ▶ `data.used`: The data used ▶ `data.mantissa`: The log data's Mantissa ▶ `data.digits`: The first digits of the data
s.o.data	A data frame with: ▶ `data.second.order`: The differences of the ordered data ▶ `data.second.order.digits`: The first digits of the second-order analysis
Bfd	A data frame with: ▶ `digits`: The groups of digits analyzed ▶ `data.dist`: The distribution of the first digits of the data ▶ `data.second.order.dist`: The distribution of the first digits of the second-order analysis ▶ `benford.dist`: The theoretical Benford distribution ▶ `data.second.order.dist.freq`: The frequency distribution of the first digits of the second-order analysis ▶ `data.dist.freq`: The frequency distribution of the first digits of the data ▶ `benford.dist.freq`: the theoretical Benford frequency distribution ▶ `benford.so.dist.freq`: The theoretical Benford frequency distribution of the second order analysis ▶ `data.summation`: The summation of the data values grouped by first digits ▶ `abs.excess.summation`: The absolute excess summation of the data values grouped by first digits ▶ `difference`: The difference between the data and Benford frequencies ▶ `squared.diff`: The chi-squared difference between the data and Benford frequencies ▶ `absolute.diff`: The absolute difference between the data and Benford frequencies

Mantissa	A data frame with: ▸ `mean.mantissa`: The mean of the Mantissa ▸ `var.mantissa`: The variance of the Mantissa ▸ `ek.mantissa`: The excess kurtosis of the Mantissa ▸ `sk.mantissa`: The skewness of the Mantissa
MAD	The mean absolute deviation
distortion.factor	The distortion factor
Stats	List of `htest` class statistics: ▸ `chisq`: Pearson's chi-squared test ▸ `mantissa.arc.test`: Mantissa Arc Test

In step 2, we plot the test results. Running plot on the object resulting from the `benford()` function will result in a plot showing the following (from upper-left corner to bottom-right corner):

- ▸ First digit distribution
- ▸ Results of the second-order test
- ▸ Summation distribution for each digit
- ▸ Results of the chi-squared test
- ▸ Summation differences

If you look carefully at these plots, you will understand which digits show a distribution significantly different from the one expected by the Benford law. In order to have a sounder base for our consideration, we need to look at the suspects table, showing absolute differences between expected and observed frequencies. This is what we will do in the next step.

In step 3, we highlight suspects digits. Using `suspectsTable()` we can easily discover which digits present the greater deviation from the expected distribution.

Looking at the suspects table, we can see that number 5 shows up as the first variable within our table. In the next step, we will focus our attention on the orders with amounts that have this digit as the first digit.

In step 4, we define a function to extrapolate the first digit from each amount. This function leverages the `substr()` function from the `stringr()` package and extracts the first digit from the number passed to it as an argument.

In step 5, we add a new column to the investigated dataset, where the first digit is extrapolated.

In step 6, we filter amounts starting with the suspected digit.

After applying the left function to our sequence of amounts, we can now filter the dataset, retaining only rows whose amounts have 5 as the first digit. We will now be able to perform analytical testing procedures on those items.

Measuring customer retention using cohort analysis in R

Within the e-commerce field, customer retention metrics can be considered crucial for several reasons. Among these, the virtual absence of a barrier to entry for competitors in the virtual arena makes online sellers very willing to build an enduring relationship with their customers.

This recipe gives you a straightforward way to compute retention metrics within the R environment.

From the possible methods available for these tasks, we will use one from the family of cohort methods.

In this method, customers are divided into homogenous groups (that is, cohorts) that share relevant segmentation attributes, such as sex or age.

Purchases made by those groups are monitored monthly over a period of time, and a retention rate is calculated each month using the following formula:

retention rate = (number of customers purchasing in a given month)/(number of customers within the cohort at the starting point)

Getting ready

This recipe is not going to leverage any particular package, apart from the `ggplot2` package. In this recipe, we will build our own derived variables, leveraging the power of vector-based R code.

Install the `ggplot2` package:

```
install.packages("ggplot2")
library(ggplot2)
```

Our example will be based on a synthetic `cohort` dataset, based on four cohorts: one for older people, one for younger people, one for men, and the last one for women.

Let's create the dataset with the following script:

```
elder_cohort <-
c(10567,9763,8327,8318,7108,6280,6279,5873,4986,3296,2986,1357)

younger_cohort <-
c(25000,24500,24324,19500,15078,11879,10856,10543,10234,9678,8542,
6321 )

total <- elder_cohort+younger_cohort

women_cohort <- total - total*0.46

men_cohort <- total - women_cohort

cohort_dataset <-
data.frame(rbind(elder_cohort,younger_cohort,women_cohort,
men_cohort))

colnames(cohort_dataset) <- c(seq(1:12))
```

Our dataset will now look like this:

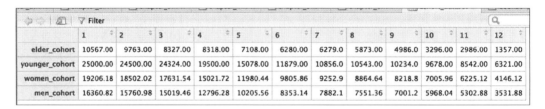

	1	2	3	4	5	6	7	8	9	10	11	12
elder_cohort	10567.00	9763.00	8327.00	8318.00	7108.00	6280.00	6279.0	5873.00	4986.0	3296.00	2986.00	1357.00
younger_cohort	25000.00	24500.00	24324.00	19500.00	15078.00	11879.00	10856.0	10543.00	10234.0	9678.00	8542.00	6321.00
women_cohort	19206.18	18502.02	17631.54	15021.72	11980.44	9805.86	9252.9	8864.64	8218.8	7005.96	6225.12	4146.12
men_cohort	16360.82	15760.98	15019.46	12796.28	10205.56	8353.14	7882.1	7551.36	7001.2	5968.04	5302.88	3531.88

How to do it...

1. Compute retention rates for each cohort:

   ```
   retention_younger <- younger_cohort/sum(younger_cohort)

   retention_elder   <- elder_cohort/sum(elder_cohort)

   retention_women   <- women_cohort/sum(women_cohort)

   retention_men     <- men_cohort/sum(men_cohort)
   ```

2. Create a unique dataset for all rates:

   ```
   retention_rates <- rbind(retention_younger,retention_
   elder,retention_women,
   retention_men)

   colnames(retention_rates) <- c(seq(1:12))
   ```

3. Plot retention rates:

```
retention_plot <- ggplot() + geom_line(aes(x =
seq(1:12),retention_younger, colour = "younger")) +
geom_line(aes(x = seq(1:12),retention_elder,colour =
"elder")) + geom_line(aes(x = seq(1:12),retention_women,
colour = "women")) + geom_line(aes(x = seq(1:12),
retention_men, colour = "men"))
retention_plot
```

How it works...

In step 1, there is a given structure for our dataset, so it is easy to compute the retention rate for each customer. This is done for each month with the lines of code that are provided and results in 12 ratios for each cohort.

In step 2, all retention rate vectors are now joined within one dataset, which will serve as a base for our plot.

In step 3, the retention_plot parameter is a ggplot2 plot built by starting with a blank layer, namely the ggplot() function, and four geom_line() layers, one for each cohort.

Refer to the *Adding text to a ggplot2 plot at a custom location* recipe in *Chapter 3, Basic Visualization Techniques*, which provides a good introduction to these plots.

Making a recommendation engine

Recommendation engines are a powerful way to boost sales on e-commerce websites, since they allow us to suggest to customers products that are likely to meet their preferences.

These suggestions are produced by looking at previous purchases (or wish lists and visited products) and comparing them with other customers and their purchases.

Basically, recommendation engines state that if you bought those products, you are similar to these other customers who also bought these products. So, probably, you will like these products as well.

Getting ready

In this recipe, we will compute the cosine measure of a matrix in order to measure similarity of vectors composing the matrix.

The lsa package provides a specific cosine() function for this purpose. In order to use it, we first have to install and load the package:

```
install.packages("lsa")
library(lsa)
```

Our recommendation engine will be applied to a data frame that stores movie reviews from five critics, ranging from 1 to 4.

Let's create the `data.frame` list with the following script:

```
reviews <- data.frame("movie" =
c("the_chronicles_of_narnia","star_wars_IV","star_wars_VI",
"beautiful_mind"),
  "Thomas" = c(1,4,4,2),
  "Jannine" = c(3,2,4,4),
  "Francis"  = c(2.4,3,2,1),
  "Mary" = c(3,2,4,3),
  "Zachary" = c(0,2,0,4))
```

How to do it...

1. Compute the cosine similarity measure between critics:

    ```
    similarity_matrix <- cosine(as.matrix(reviews[,2:6]))
    ```

2. Transpose the original data frame list:

    ```
    t_reviews <- as.data.frame(t(reviews))

    colnames(t_reviews) <-
    c("the_chronicles_of_narnia","star_wars_IV","star_wars_VI",
    "beautiful_mind")

    t_reviews[,1]        <- as.numeric(t_reviews[,1])
    t_reviews[,2]        <- as.numeric(t_reviews[,2])
    t_reviews[,3]        <- as.numeric(t_reviews[,3])
    t_reviews[,4]        <- as.numeric(t_reviews[,4])
    ```

3. Define the weighted score by multiplying reviews for the similarity score of each critic with Zachary:

    ```
    weighted_scores <- similarity_matrix[,5]*t_reviews[,1:4]
    ```

4. Define movies that Zachary will probably like:

    ```
    zachary_suggestions <- colSums(weighted_scores)

    > zachary_suggestions
    the_chronicles_of_narnia                star_wars_IV
    star_wars_VI                    beautiful_mind
                      12.615616                        8.010968
          10.432623                    11.751864
    ```

According to our recommendation engine, Zachary is most likely to appreciate `the_chronicles_of_narnia` from the movies provided.

Performing time series decomposition using the stl() function

Nearly every phenomenon can be represented as a time series.

It is therefore not surprising that time series analysis is one of most popular topics within data-science communities.

As is often the case, R provides a great tool for time-series decomposition, starting with the `stl()` function provided within base R itself. This function will be the base of our recipe.

Getting ready

This recipe will mainly use the `stl()` function, which implements the `Loess()` method for time-series decomposition.

Using this method, we are able to separate a time series into three different parts:

- ▶ **Trend component**: This highlights the core trend of the phenomenon if perturbations and external influence were not in place
- ▶ **Seasonal component**: This is linked to cyclical influences
- ▶ **Remainder**: This groups all non-modeled (in hypothesis random) effects

As mentioned earlier, this function is provided with every R base version, and we therefore don't need to install any additional packages.

A dataset, named **nottem**, is provided with the R base as well, and is composed and defined by R documentation as a time series object containing average air temperatures at Nottingham Castle, in degrees Fahrenheit, for 20 years.

You can easily inspect it in the viewer pane by running the `View()` function on it:

```
View(nottem)
```

How to do it...

1. Apply the `stl()` function to the `nottem` dataset:
   ```
   nottem_decomposition <- stl(nottem, s.window = "periodic")
   ```

2. Plot the decomposition results:
   ```
   plot(nottem_decomposition)
   ```

Let's take a look at the following image:

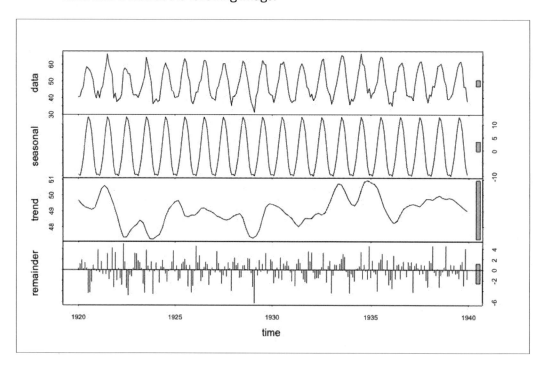

3. Focus on the trend component:

```
plot(nottem_decomposition$time.series[,2],ylab =
"trend_component")
```

Let's take a look at the following graph:

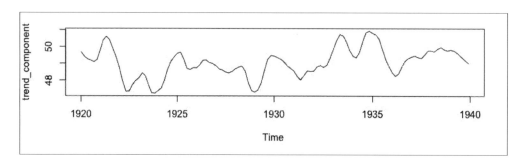

Exploring time series forecasting with forecast()

The most logical next step after understanding a time series' features and trends is trying to forecast its future development.

As one would imagine, R provides optimal tools to perform this task.

In this recipe, we will leverage the extremely popular `forecast` package by Professor Rob J Hyndman. The package provides an always increasing number of tools for performing univariate time series forecasting.

You can find out more on the package on Prof. Hyndman's personal site at `http://robjhyndman.com/software/forecast/`.

Getting ready

As stated earlier, the only package needed to perform this recipe is the `forecast` package. We therefore need to install it and load it:

```
install.packages("forecast")
library(forecast)
```

How to do it...

1. Apply the `stl()` function to the `nottem` dataset:

   ```
   nottem_decomposition <- stl(nottem, s.window = "periodic")
   ```

2. Forecast five more years:

   ```
   forecast <- forecast(nottem_decomposition,h = 5)
   ```

3. Plot the forecasted values:

   ```
   plot(forecast(nottem_decomposition))
   ```

   Let's take a look at the following graph:

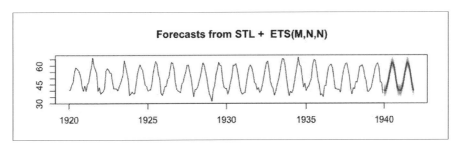

In this plot, you will see a section highlighted in blue. I am sure you have already guessed it; the blue section is exactly what we have been looking for in this recipe, that is, forecasted values.

Tracking stock movements using the quantmod package

An affordable and time-saving way to download and store stock prices can be considered a prerequisite for every future analysis on financial portfolio data.

The `quantmod` package offers R users a really convenient way to perform this task. Complete documentation for the package is available at `http://www.quantmod.com`.

Quantmod, through the `getSymbols()` function, lets you establish a direct connection with financial data sources such as:

- Yahoo Finance
- Google Finance
- `www.oanda.com`
- Federal Reserve economic data

This recipe will leverage the `getSymbols()` function to download Apple's stock quotations. A proper candle and bar chart will then be produced.

Getting ready

As you would expect, we first need to install and load the package:

```
install.packages("quantmod")
library('quantmod')
```

How to do it...

1. Download data from Yahoo Finance:

   ```
   getSymbols("AAPL")
   ```

2. Plot your data on candlechart:

   ```
   candleChart(AAPL, subset = 'last 1 year')
   ```

Let's take a look at the following chart:

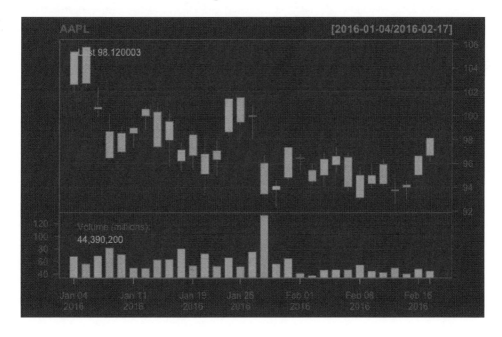

3. Plot your data on a bar chart:

```
barChart(AAPL, subset = 'last 1 year')
```

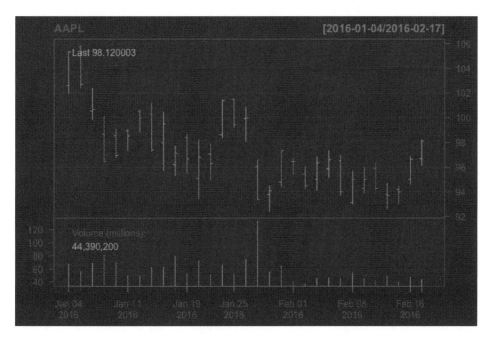

Optimizing portfolio composition and maximising returns with the Portfolio Analytics package

Portfolio optimization is basically composed of four main steps:

- ▸ Definition of portfolio components and past quotations
- ▸ Definition of portfolio constrains, for instance, in term of diversification or maximum loss
- ▸ Definition of objective to be optimized, usually in terms of returns
- ▸ Definition of optimal percentage composition, given constraints and objectives

In this recipe, we will employ `PortfolioAnaltycs` and some other packages by joining together functionalities from different packages in order to provide a convenient and straightforward way to compose a financial portfolio.

The recipe workflow will be as follows:

- ▸ Downloading stock prices
- ▸ Definition of portfolio constraints and objectives
- ▸ Actual portfolio optimization

Getting ready

In this recipe, we will join together powerful functions from different packages.

First of all, we will download stock quotations from Yahoo Finance by leveraging the `quantmod` package.

The downloaded information will then be grouped within a `portfolio` object and an optimal portfolio composition will be computed, employing functions from the `PortfolioAnalytics`, `ROI`, and `Deoptim` packages. The `ROI` package will be employed in its extended version, thanks to the `glpk` and `quadrprog` plugins.

In order to add those plugins, we will first have to install the `Rcmdr` package.

Summing it all, you will have to run the following code to install and load the required packages:

```
library(DEoptim)
library(ROI)
library(ROI.plugin.glpk)
library(ROI.plugin.quadprog)
```

```
library(plugin)
library(quantmod)
library(PortfolioAnalytics)
```

How to do it...

1. Download data and store it in a portfolio data frame:

```
stocks <- getSymbols(c("FCA","AAPL","GOOG"), env = sp500,
    from = as.Date("2015-01-01"),
    to = as.Date("2015-10-31"))
FCA <- sp500$FCA
FCA <- get("FCA",envir = sp500)
FCA <- with(sp500, FCA)
AAPL <- sp500$AAPL
AAPL <- get("AAPL",envir = sp500)
AAPL <- with(sp500,AAPL)
GOOG <- sp500$GOOG
GOOG <- get("GOOG",envir = sp500)
GOOG <- with(sp500,GOOG)
FCA  <- as.data.frame(FCA)
FCA  <- FCA$FCA.Adjusted
GOOG <- as.data.frame(GOOG)
GOOG <- GOOG$GOOG.Adjusted
AAPL <- as.data.frame(AAPL)
AAPL <- AAPL$AAPL.Adjusted


portfolio <- data.frame(FCA,GOOG,AAPL)
```

2. Change the portfolio row names by setting them equal to dates:

```
row.names(portfolio) <- seq.Date(from = as.Date("2015-01-01"),
to = as.Date("2015-01-01") + nrow(portfolio)-1,by ="days")
```

3. Initialize a `portfolio` object by passing to it stock names:

```
portfolio_obj <- portfolio.spec(assets = colnames(portfolio))
```

4. Add a minimum and a maximum composition constraint:

```
portfolio_obj <- add.constraint(portfolio = portfolio_obj,
  type = "box",
  min = c(0.01, 0.28, 0.1),
  max = c(0.4, 0.5, 0.25))
```

5. Add a diversification constraint:

```
portfolio_obj <- add.constraint(portfolio = portfolio_obj,
type = "diversification", div_target = 0.7)
```

6. Specify mean return maximization as an objective:

```
portfolio_obj <- add.objective(portfolio = portfolio_obj,
type = 'return', name = 'mean')
```

7. Compute optimal portfolio composition, given the constraints and objectives:

```
optimal_portfolio_obj <- optimize.portfolio( R = portfolio,
portfolio = portfolio_obj, optimize_method = "ROI", trace =
TRUE)

print(optimal_portfolio_obj)


> print(optimal_portfolio_obj)

*********************************

PortfolioAnalytics Optimization

*********************************


Call:

optimize.portfolio(R = portfolio, portfolio = portfolio_obj,
optimize_method = "ROI", trace = TRUE)


Optimal Weights:
 FCA GOOG AAPL
0.25 0.50 0.25


Objective Measure:
 mean
322.5
```

Forecasting the stock market

In this recipe, we will develop a step-by-step 2-year forecast of the **Fiat-Chrysler Automotive** stock price.

This task will be accomplished by applying the Arima modeling technique to FCA stock time series.

Arima (**Autoregressive integrated moving average**) models basically involve the estimation of an autoregressive model and a moving average, employed to estimate both the stochastic part and the underlying trend.

Getting ready

This recipe is mainly based on the `tseries` package and `forecast` package, the first for Arima model fitting and the second for prediction of future values. We will also need the `quantmod` package in order to download stock data from Yahoo Finance.

We therefore need to install and load these three packages:

```
install.packages(c("tseries","forecast","quantmod"))

library(tseries)

library(forecast)

library(quantmod)
```

How to do it...

1. Download data:

```
sp500 <- new.env()

stocks <- getSymbols(c("FCA"), env = sp500,
   from = as.Date("2015-01-01"),
   to = as.Date("2015-10-31"))

FCA <- sp500$FCA

FCA <- get("FCA",envir = sp500)

FCA <- with(sp500, FCA)

FCA  <- as.data.frame(FCA)

FCA  <- FCA$FCA.Adjusted
```

2. Compute percentage log differences:

    ```
    time_series <- 100 * diff(log(FCA))
    ```

3. Derive a train dataset:

    ```
    time_series_train <- time_series[1:(0.9 *
    length(time_series))] # Train dataset
    ```

4. Train an Arima model on the train dataset:

    ```
    arima_fit       <- arima(time_series_train, order = c(2, 0, 2))
    arima_forecast <- forecast(arima_fit)
    ```

5. Plot a forecast:

    ```
    plot(arima_forecast, main = "ARMA forecasts FCA returns")
    ```

    Let's take a look at the following graph:

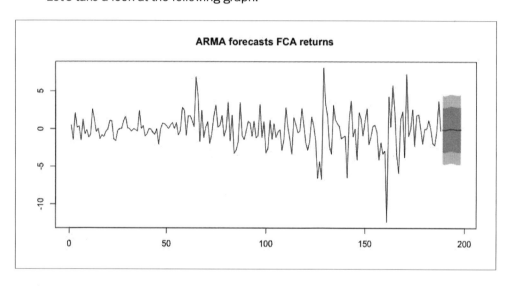

7
Developing Static Reports

In this chapter, we will cover the following topics:

- ► Using one markup language for all types of documents – `rmarkdown`
- ► Writing and styling PDF documents with RStudio
- ► Writing wonderful tufte handouts with the `tufte` package and `rmarkdown`
- ► Sharing your code and plots with slides
- ► Curating a blog through RStudio

Introduction

In this chapter, we will provide tools for the last part of your data-analysis project: result sharing. This is a relevant phase since your work will give no added value if you do not effectively communicate it.

You know this is true, but how do you do it?

The answer to this question can be split into two parts:

- ► The marketing part
- ► The technical part

Let's first briefly address the first part, since the second one will be addressed throughout the chapter. Talking about the marketing part, I refer to all those strategies and activities you perform to sell your product better. Your product is your job, and if you don't sell it properly, nobody is going to buy it and you would have wasted your time.

This is not the right place to address the point in a proper and complete way, but let me stress at least two points:

▸ Do not show data, tell a story with it: I know you are really proud of having found a unexpected correlation between that variable and your revenues, but just showing a correlation coefficient will not thrill anyone (except you). You should rather ask, "What story does it tell? Does it mean we can influence our revenues by pushing hard on that given variable?" OK, if you think so, show it. Say aloud that "by increasing expenditure on this, we can grow our revenue by 25 percent." Isn't this better than a correlation coefficient?

▸ Always ask yourself, "So what?": When you are crafting your report, you should always imagine that you have someone in front of you who asks, "So what?" If you are able to answer this question in a convincing way, you are preparing to win (and sell). Let's try it. We say, "We found that the number of injuries suffered in a year by a person is strongly correlated to his age (surprise!), which is a significant variable for our retention rate." The impolite man says, "So what?" We reply, "So, we can reduce our research costs by avoiding acquiring data about injuries". So that's the point: expenditure cuts!

Let's face the technical part now. In the modern world, the more precious resource is time. It is therefore considered a waste of time copying and pasting results from your job into a file external to your coding environment, and copying and pasting it again when even a small detail changes.

This process can also be considered error prone. Within your copy-and-paste activity, you can bet a considerable sum on forgetting to update some values and sending your boss outdated numbers. This, as we know, is not a pleasant experience.

This chapter will help you avoid such unpleasant scenarios and give you great tools to develop reports on your work directly from the place where it was produced: RStudio. In this chapter, you will learn how to develop reports directly by embedding numbers, plots, and data frames from your code. When you change the code and outputs change, your report will change by itself.

Doesn't it sound like a dream?

Our best friend in this chapter, and part of the next one as well, will be **rmarkdown**, a powered markup language. It lets you embed and execute pieces of R code within documents written in the Markdown language, the popular markup language created by Joghn Gruber in 2004. We will employ rmarkdown in this chapter to write reports, PDF documents, and tufte handouts. We will also use rmarkdown to curate a blog directly from your favorite IDE.

Using one markup language for all types of documents – rmarkdown

As mentioned earlier, Markdown is a popular markup language developed by John Gruber.

This language is based on the principle of the supremacy of plain text documents over all other kinds of format.

Plain text is the base for any subsequent kind of manipulation and will be always readable without any particular software. This will let your work be usable and understandable for years to come and will not let you become the hostage of a particular software provider.

Rmarkdown integrates the Markdown language with some facilities for R code integration, which lets you show results from running R code, such as plots or tables, in a Markdown document.

Getting ready

Let's warm up by installing and loading the required packages:

```
install.packages("rmarkdown")
install.packages("knitr")
library(rmarkdown)
library(knitr)
```

How to do it...

1. Create a new R Markdown document:

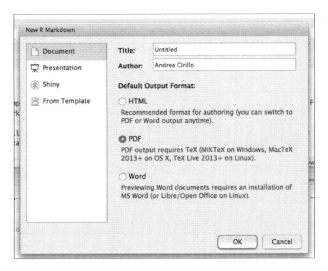

2. Remove the default content from the document, except for YAML parameters, as we don't want to be bound by the already available default content. Just go and delete it. The only part I ask you to preserve is the first chunk of text enclosed within two '—' tokens.

3. Specify the YAML parameters to obtain the table of contents.

   To add the table of contents, you have to remove this line:

   ```
   output: html_document
   ```

   Insert at the same point the following lines:

   ```
   output:
    html_document:
     toc: yes
   ```

   You should be aware that YAML is in some way "space sensitive." This means that the number of indentation spaces will be considered during document file rendering to understand the meaning of the full line of code.

   In our example, we have to place one space before `html_document` and two spaces before `toc: yes`. The first space will let us read `html_document` as a value of the `output` parameter, while the two spaces before `toc: yes` will signify that this token is a value of the `html_document:` argument.

4. Add a setup chunk:

   ```
   ```{r setup, include=FALSE}
   knitr::opts_chunk$set(echo = TRUE)
   library(knitr)
   ```
   ```

5. Add a main title:

   ```
   #main title
   ```

6. Add a structure:

   ```
   ## first paragraph


   ## second paragraph


   ## first subparagraph
   ```

7. Navigate the document structure using the outline viewer:

8. Add a plot:

```
```{r plot, echo= FALSE}
plot(iris$Sepal.Length,iris$Petal.Width)
```
```

9. Add a table from a dataset:

```
```{r kable, echo= FALSE}
kable(iris[1:10,])
```
```

10. Give the possibility to fold the code.

    Add the following to the `yaml` parameters:

    ```
    code_folding: hide
    ```

11. Add a value within the text from the `r` elaboration.

    In an R Markdown document, it is also possible to expose a value that comes from running some R code. In our example, we will embed the number of rows composing the `iris` dataset (150, if you are wondering). Two mandatory parts for embedding R output within a document are the `` `r `` token at the beginning and the `` ` `` token at the end.

    ```
    `r nrow(iris)`
    ```

12. Add a link to external resources:

    ```
    [link to the R project website](https://www.r-project.org)
    ```

13. Add a link to internal resources:

    ```
    [link to chapter 7 codefile](chapter_7.R)
    ```

14. Embed a picture:

    ```
    ![image](aclogo.png)
    ```

15. Render your document.

You can render you document through the knit control on the upper bar, or simply use *Ctrl + Shift + K*.

How it works...

In step 1, the R Markdown is perfectly integrated in the RStudio environment. Creating a new R Markdown report just requires you to select the **File** menu and the **New R Markdown report** option.

In step 2, we just require you to delete the default content of the document. There is not much to say here, am I right?

In step 3, the `yaml` parameters are used during the rendering phase (which you will start in the last step of this recipe) to set some attributes of the document.

With an acceptable approximation, we can say that within the `yaml` chunk, we set the document's metadata.

Adding a table of contents requires you to modify the `output:html_document` statement to let it receive more arguments to render the output.

Be aware that other parameters can be set for the HTML document. You can set them from the output options, which you can access in the following menu:

It's even possible to specify a different kind of output from HTML, directly from the knit menu:

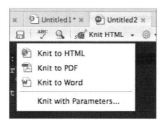

Refer to the _Writing and styling PDF documents with RStudio_ recipe for more details on PDF `outputs.lòk.`

In step 4, the question to ask is, "What is a setup chunk?" I am sure you are guessing right. A setup chunk is a chunk of R code used to define the general settings of your document.

It is in no way different from other chunks, but it is a best practice to have all preliminary activities necessary for your analysis development in one place.

For instance you can place within this chunk package installation and loading, data frame import, code loading, and so on.

In step 5, we add a main title. This step and the following one will let you add a structure to your document, dividing it into paragraphs and subparagraphs, all starting with a principal title.

If you have some familiarity with HTML code, it will help you in the following table, which relates the HTML headers' node tokens to the corresponding R Markdown code:

Html node	R Markdown	Output
`<h1></h1>`	`#`	`Title`
`<h2></h2>`	`##`	`Title`
`<h3></h3>`	`###`	`Title`
`<h4></h4>`	`####`	`Title`
`<h5></h5>`	`#####`	`Title`
`<h6></h6>`	`######`	`Title`

Adding a number for # greater than six will simply result in the # tokens not being shown and the following text being reproduced as body text.

In step 6, you can define a structure for your document using the heading shown in the previous step.

In step 7, among the features introduced with the 0.99 version, which deserves a place of honor, is certainly the outline viewer for R Markdown documents.

This viewer produces a navigable index for your document, letting you quickly understand the structure it is assuming.

To achieve this, the RStudio IDE looks for the previously introduced # tokens and for chunks of R code.

In step 8 we add a plot. The core feature of R Markdown is embedding embeds the results from an R environment within a markdown document.

> ▸ Even if our example here is a really basic one, it lets you completely understand the power of this feature

You can embed the results of R code computations, such as plots or tables, within your documents surrounding the piece of R code we want to run with the following tokens:

```
```{r name_of_the_chunck}
```
```

You can now decide some parameters to fine-tune the appearance of elaboration results. The ones you will more likely use are as follows:

> ▸ `Echo FALSE/TRUE` specifies whether results from the elaboration, different from plots, should be shown within the document.
>
> ▸ `Warnings FALSE/TRUE` should be set to `true` if you want R warnings to be printed out (for instance, warnings on package loading).
>
> ▸ `Fig.caption` is the caption of your plot, which sets the caption to be shown under plots (if any) produced from the chunk of code. Be aware of setting `fig_caption = TRUE` under `html_document` within `yaml` parameters to make captions visible. See step 3 for more information on `yaml` parameters.

You can get a sense of all the available settings by writing:

```
```{r name_of_chunk,
```

After inputting " , " RStudio will show you a list of possible settings.

You can find a complete and explained list of possible settings on the website of `yihui xie`, the author and maintainer of the `knitr` package, which is the base of the `rmarkdown` package. You can find the website at `http://yihui.name/knitr/options/`.
```

In step 9, we add a table from a dataset. One of the most annoying things in markdown is probably table creation. You have to input them cell by cell, dividing your cells by "|".

Fortunately, R Markdown doesn't require you to do this, but rather provides a really easy and convenient way of showing your data frames as well as formatted tables, simply by calling the `kable()` function.

In step 10, we provide the ability to fold the code. To let a code fold/unfold, the controls appear in the upper-right corner of your document. You can add the following parameter within the `yaml` section:

code_folding: hide

This will make the following control appear:

Using this control, the reader will be able to specify whether pieces of code will be shown within the document or not. This control can significantly enhance the readability of your document, especially if long chunks of code are introduced within the text.

In step 11, we add a value within the text that comes from from R elaboration. This is a really nice feature of R Markdown. It greatly broadens its horizons. Be aware that even those small scripts will have access to the general document environment and will therefore be able to use all objects and functions within this environment.

In step 12, we add a link to external resources. Including a link to external sources is useful, especially when writing documents to be published online. You can add an external link specifying a proper label (the text that will appear) within squared brackets and the actual link to point to between round brackets. Here is an example:

[text to show]("www.the_actual_url.com")

In step 13, we add a link to internal resources. The main difference between this step and the previous one is the relative location of the linked file. In this case, we are pointing to a file placed in the working directory of the calling file (our R Markdown document). We can therefore just specify the piece of path from the directory we are working on.

In step 14, we embed a picture. With a script not too different from the one used for links, we can embed an image, specifying the location of the image file in round brackets.

In step 15 we render the document. If everything went right, after hitting the **knit document** button, you will see a new tab appear next to the console tab. The new tab will be labeled R Markdown.

In this new tab, logs from R Markdown processing will appear, acknowledging the activities being performed by RStudio to create an HTML file from your R Markdown document.

At the end of the process, your HTML document will show up.

There's more...

Markdown is a really popular and always growing language.

You can use it in an increasing number of virtual places, from GitHub to Wordpress.

Here are some useful resources you can explore to broaden your topic knowledge:

- R Markdown official website for RStudio at `http://rmarkdown.rstudio.com`
- Markdown syntax introduction on the official markdown website at `https://daringfireball.net/projects/markdown/syntax`

Writing and styling PDF documents with RStudio

Even in the era of the Internet, PDF documents are a really convenient way to share your results.

That is probably why RStudio provides you with an easy way to create PDF documents from your R Markdown documents.

Getting ready

To produce PDF documents from our device, we first need to install the latest distribution of a convenient LaTeX engine.

On Apple devices, we suggest downloading the latest **Mactex** version from `http://tug.org/mactex/mactex-download.html`, while Windows users can download **Miktext** from `http://miktex.org/download`.

Linux users can use **Texlive**, which can be found at `https://www.tug.org/texlive/quickinstall.html`.

How to do it...

1. Create a new R Markdown document, specifying PDF as output:

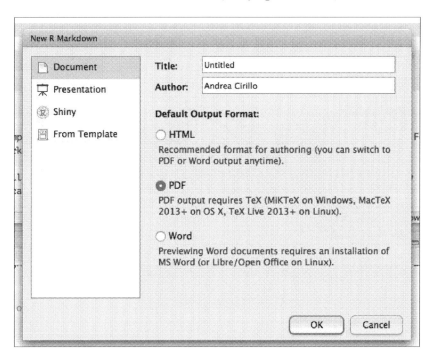

2. Render your PDF document.

    Rendering your PDF document simply involves hitting the **Knit PDF** button:

There's more...

In the R Markdown framework, PDF is just one of the possible output formats. All possible customizations available within the R Markdown format are available. Refer to the *Using one markup language for all types of documents – rmarkdown* recipe for an extensive introduction to them.

Writing wonderful tufte handouts with the tufte package and rmarkdown

Edward Tufte is one of most inspiring evangelists of effective data visualization of modern times.

His book on effective ways of showing data and telling stories with them has made a great impact on a lot of data-visualization tools and theories.

One of the most typical features of his books is the extensive use of side notes, with both images and text, to further explain concepts introduced in the main body text.

Given the popularity of this layout, R Markdown offers the possibility of creating documents containing side notes, letting you even introduce pieces of R code or plots generated from R code as side notes.

Getting ready

Before working with tufte handouts, we have to install and load the latest version of R Markdown on our computer (refer to the first recipe of this chapter for further information on markdown).

This can be easily done by running the following code:

```
install.packages("rmarkdown")
library(rmarkdown)
```

How to do it...

1. Create a new tufte handout.

   First select a new R Makdown:

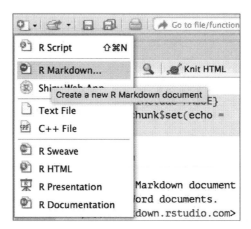

Then, look for the tufte handout in the from the **Template:** tab:

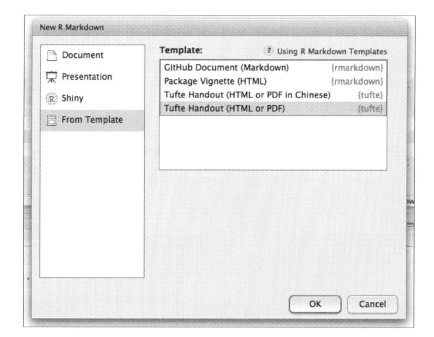

This will produce your tufte handout, already populated with some explicative content.

2. Preview the handout.

   To see how your handout looks, you just have to hit the **run** button above your file.

   You can render your document through the knit HTML control on the upper bar, or simply by using *Ctrl + Shift + K*.

3. Add a side note.

   Side notes are the core feature of the tufte layout. You can add one in a way similar to the one used for R code chunk insertion:

   ```` ```{marginfigure} ````

   We know from _ the first fundamental theorem of calculus _ that for x in $[a, b]$:

   ```
   $$\frac{d}{dx}\left( \int_{a}^{x} f(u)\,du\right)=f(x).$$
   ```

   Be aware that the first line (or the top of the plot) of your side note will be aligned to the line of the main body, which is immediately before the ```` ```{marginfigure} ```` token.
   ```

4. Add a quote:

   ```
   > Essentially, all models are wrong
   
   > but some are useful
   
   > `r tufte::quote_footer('--- George E.P. Box')`
   ```

5. Save your handout as HTML and knit your handout.

You can render your document through the knit HTML control on the upper bar or simply by using *Ctrl + Shift + K*.

Once your handout is rendered, hit the **Open** button in the browser. When in the browser, save your page. This can be done with *cmd + S* on Mac and *Shift + F12* on Windows.

There's more...

Within tufte handouts, all features available for R Markdown documents are available.

Refer to the *Using one markup language for all types of documents – rmarkdown* recipe.

Sharing your code and plots with slides

We live in slide times.

An ever-increasing portion of our knowledge is deposited on those horizontal decks, usually written in really unreadable 8-point characters.

Even if criticism on the bad use of slides is growing (see, for instance, the great book *Presentation Zen* by Garr Reynolds) at the moment, you will still have to face that fatal request, "Could you prepare a deck on that job you have done?."

So, why miss the opportunity to do it directly within your coding best friend, RStudio?

Here, I will show you how to prepare a nice deck of slides within the IDE, leveraging the R Markdown language once again.

How to do it...

1. Create a new R Markdown presentation:

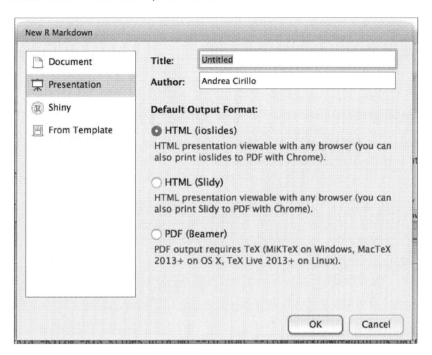

2. Preview your slides.

   You can preview you slides through the knit HTML control on the upper bar or simply by using *Ctrl + Shift + K*.

3. Add a logo to your slides:

```
---
title: "slides"
author: "Andrea Cirillo"
date: "27 February 2016"
output:
  ioslides_presentation:
    logo: aclogo.png
---
```

4. Enable and add captions to your figures.

    Enabling captions on figures involves specifying it within the metadata of your slides, where we put the logo source path. The caption option is specified using the following code:

    ```
    fig_caption: yes
    ```

    You can now add a caption to a figure, making it explicit within the chunk containing the plot, as shown in the following chunk:

    ```
    ```{r pressure, fig.cap = "pressure plot"}
    plot(pressure)
    ```
    ```

5. Save your slides as portable HTML.

You can render your slides through the knit HTML control on the upper bar or simply by using *Ctrl + Shift + K*.

Once your slides are rendered, hit the **Open** button in the browser, and when in the browser, save your page. This can be done with *cmd + S* on Mac and *Shift + F12* on Windows.

Curating a blog through RStudio

So now you do all your analytical work in RStudio. You create reports about your job in RStudio, either as PDF documents or HTML files. You even produce slides in RStudio.

Excluding asking RStudio to pay your bills, what more could you expect from this IDE?

Perhaps producing websites to share your work on the World Wide Web.

Well, RStudio actually can do it!

This recipe will show you how to produce and maintain a blog directly from RStudio.

We will see how to produce a website composed of R Markdown files and structured in the following recipe.

Getting ready

To perform some of the activities in this recipe, we will employ the wget utility, which is available both for Unix and Windows OS.

We will use it to download and save HTML files from the Web.

You can find information on wget installation for Unix OS at http://www.cyberciti.biz/faq/howto-freebsd-installing-gnu-wget-command-port/.

For Windows OS, I suggest that you visit the page by Richard Baxter at https://builtvisible.com/download-your-website-with-wget/.

In this recipe, we will interact with an online GitHub repository using a command-line session. Within RStudio, it is also possible to obtain same results linking your project to the online repository, and handling commits and pushing through the apposite Git pane in the top-right corner.

If you wish to know more about this, I suggest that you go through the *Using GitHub with RStudio* recipe in *Chapter 5, Power Programming with R*.

How to do it...

1. Create an RStudio project for your blog.

   OK, this is easy. Just create a new empty RStudio project.

2. Create a github.io repository.

   Some years ago, GitHub started offering a free website-hosting service, perfectly integrated with its Git repository hosting service. This service is named GitHub Pages and has got its own website at https://pages.github.com.

   For our purpose, we just have to create an empty repository (don't worry, we are going to fill it later) that has the same name as your GitHub user account, for instance, andreacirilloac/github.io.

Navigate to the following link (assuming you are already logged in to GitHub) to create a new repository, `github.com/new`:

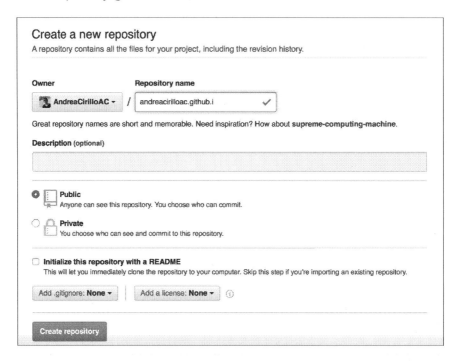

3.   Open your RStudio project and launch a terminal session.

RStudio comes with a proper menu control to open a shell/terminal session. Just go and hit it:

4. Authenticate on Git from the terminal.

   You now need to remotely authenticate to GitHub from your remote desktop, run the following command to accomplish this task (substituting `andreacirilloac` with your GitHub account name):

   ```
   git config --global user.name "AndreaCirilloAC"
   ```

5. Execute the following command:

   ```
   git config --global user.email "andreacirilloac@gmail.com"
   ```

6. Copy the repository URL.

   In your online repository, you will find the URL of your repository. Just go and copy it while I wait for you here:

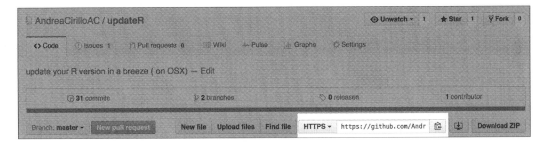

7. Clone the repository.

   Now you can make a copy of your online repository on your local machine, that is, you can clone your repository, paste the previously copied HTTPS address in the following command, and run it on the shell/terminal session:

   ```
   git clone https://github.com/AndreaCirilloAC/andreacirilloac.
   github.io.git
   ```

8. Download the RStudio Markdown website template.

   The people at RStudio provided a website template to help us get started with this really nice way of blogging. Taking advantage of their kindness just requires us to download the template using `wget` within our `terminal/shell` session:

   ```
   wget /rstudio/rmarkdown-website/raw/master/_navbar.html
   ```

   This will add the template to our current directory, which is also our RStudio project directory.

9. Open the `.gitignore` file and add the `.rproj` file.

   `.gitignore` files are used to let the Git system know which files shouldn't be tracked within Git.

   We can specify within this file whatever we want. However, I would recommend that you add your `.rproj` file by writing `your_rstudio_project_name.rproj` within your `.gitignore` file, which should be placed within the RStudio project.

10. Download the `makefile` blog.

    `makefile` is a file used during website building, containing relevant metadata such as the kind of output to produce.

    We can easily download it using `wget`, once again due to the courtesy of the RStudio team, from `https://github.com/rstudio/rmarkdown-website/blob/master/Makefile`.

11. Create an `output.yaml` file.

    In this step, we will create a `.yaml` file, containing data on the output we want to produce from the Markdown code, which is, in our case, an HTML file.

    Creating this file can be done using the `touch` command on the `terminal/session` if you are on a Unix OS:

    ```
    touch _output.yaml
    ```

    If you are on a Windows OS, you should instead use the following command:

    ```
    New-Item -ItemType file output.yaml
    ```

12. Add content to your `.yaml` file:

    We are now going to add content to our `.yaml` file by specifying the required kind of the output and other parameters.

    In both Unix and Windows OS, we can do this using the `echo` command and the pipe operator:

    ```
    echo "html_document:
    > self_contained: false
    > lib_dir: libs
    > " > _output.yaml
    ```

13. Create an `index.rmd` file.

    The `index.rmd` file will represent your blog home, so you can add to it all the content you would like to help your reader get oriented within the website.

    Refer to the *Using one markup language for all types of documents – rmarkdown* recipe to see how to fill and style your document.

14. Create an `about_me.rmd` file.

    This blog usually contains an about me page to introduce the website author(s).

15. Write a first post in a `first_pos.rmd` file.

16. Push your modifications to your GitHub repository.

    Push your new file to the online repository first by adding all modified files to a new commit. Then, commit and finally push from the terminal session:

    ```
    git add -a
    git commit
    git push
    ```

17. Navigate to your site.

Before actually navigating to your freshly built website, you should wait a few minutes to let the GitHub service read and build your website.

After that, your website will be up and running, and you should see it at `http://your_account_name.github.io`.

8

Dynamic Reporting and Web Application Development

In this chapter, we will cover for the following topics:

- ▶ Generating dynamic parametrized reports with R Markdown
- ▶ Developing a single-file Shiny app
- ▶ Changing a Shiny app UI based on user input
- ▶ Creating an interactive report with Shiny
- ▶ Constructing RStudio add-ins
- ▶ Sharing your work on RPubs
- ▶ Deploying your app on Amazon AWS with ramazon

Introduction

This final chapter will add some advanced communication tools to your programmer toolkit. These tools will enable you to show your analytics work in the best possible way.

We are going to deepen our knowledge of R Markdown, the RStudio version of the markup language markdown introduced in *Chapter 7, Developing Static Reports*. R Markdown integrates the core features of this language with some powerful facilities for R code integration.

This language will let us create dynamic and parametrized reports, perfect for periodical reporting activity, such as doing market surveys and audit follow-ups.

We will always meet RPubs in the results-sharing field. It is an online publication platform perfectly integrated with RStudio, which will let you publish your work directly from your favorite IDE by just hitting a button.

Finally, we will explore the ever-expanding world of Shiny, the web application framework provided by RStudio.

Within this field, we will touch upon the advanced topic of dynamic UI development based on user inputs, along with the newest improvement to the Shiny framework: RStudio add-ins. By developing add-ins, RStudio users are able to expand the functionalities of their favorite IDE. They are able to define text macros or little Shiny apps for the accomplishment of custom activities, from simple data frame subsetting to polynomial regression fitting.

Generating dynamic parametrized reports with R Markdown

This recipe will leverage R Markdown to produce parametrized reports where the user is prompted to specify arguments related to the report, and the report is then produced.

In this recipe, you will find screenshots taken from an R Markdown document.

The full document is provided within the RStudio project related to the cookbook, under the name `parametrized_report.rmd`.

Getting ready

From a technical point of view, all you need in order to perform this recipe is to install the `rmarkdown` and `knintr` packages, so let's install and load them:

```
Install.packages("rmarkdown",type = "source")
install.packages("knitr")
library(rmarkdown)
library(knitr)
```

From a practical point of view, you should quickly run through the *Using one markup language for all types of documents – rmarkdown* recipe from *Chapter 7, Developing Static Reports*. It will make you confident about using the R Markdown language.

How to do it...

1. Create a new R Markdown report.

   R Markdown reports can be easily created using the appropriate control in the upper-left corner of RStudio:

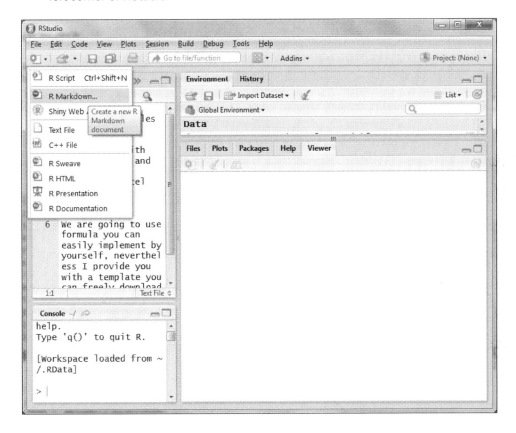

You can now select the title of your report and the type of output. Refer to the *Using one markup language for all types of documents – rmarkdown* recipe in *Chapter 7, Developing Static Reports* for further details:

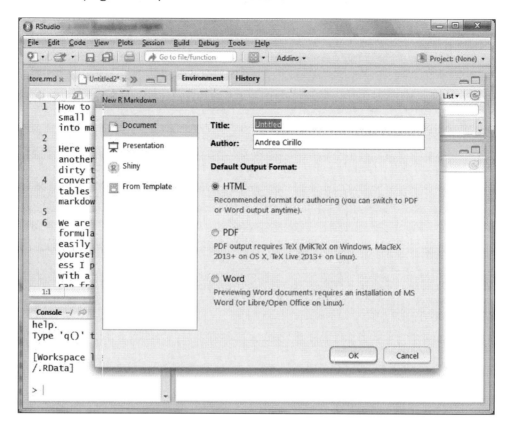

2. We then define the parameters:

```
 1  ---
 2  title: "params_report"
 3  author: "Andrea Cirillo"
 4  date: "25 February 2016"
 5  output: html_document
 6  params:
 7    stock:
 8      label:"input stock name"
 9      value: "AAPL"
10      input: "text"
11
12  ---
```

3. Next, let's define the function-calling parameters:

```r
16 - ```{r}
17    install.packages(quantmod)
18    library(quantmod)
19    params$stock
20    stock <- getSymbols(params$stock)
21    stock_data <- get(stock)
22    stock_data <- as.data.frame(stock_data)
23    plot(stock_data[,4])
24    head(stock_data[,1:3],n = 20)
25 - ```
```

4. Test your report.

   There are two ways to test your report. You can try out either of the following:

   1. Select **Knit to HTML** and select **Knit with Parameters...**:

   2. Submit the following line of code to the console:

   ```r
   rmarkdown::render("parametrized_report.Rmd", params = 'ask')
   ```

   Both alternatives will result in a window popping up, asking you to specify the value of the parameters created:

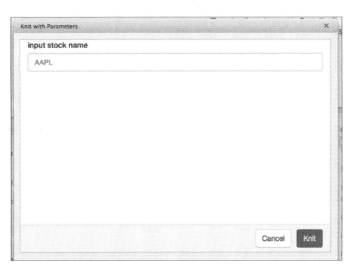

After having provided the selected value of the parameter (try for instance GOOGL instead of the default AAPL), you will have to press Knit to produce the actual report:

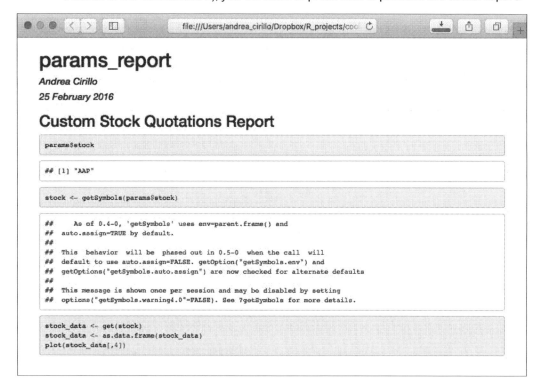

How it works...

We first created the document. Then, we actually defined the parameter we will use to interactively change our report inputs.

Parameters are defined within the `yaml` chunk, which defines some metadata for the document. It is used within the document-deployment phase to understand the kind of output you expect, whether you need a table of content, and of course, whether some parameters are to be asked to the user.

Let's have a look at the structure of our `stock` parameter:

  ▸ **Label**: This is the message the user will see. It is intended to explain what the parameter is about and how the user should define it.

  ▸ **Value**: This is the default value of our parameter.

  ▸ **Input**: This is the kind of input control shown to the user to let them select the parameter value. These controls are taken directly from the Shiny web application framework, which is explained in the *Developing a single-file Shiny app* recipe.

It is important to visualize that as parameters should be defined, all those values that are likely to change within the report, such as the cutoff date, geographical area, family of product, and relevant process to be investigated can't be hard coded within the report.

Once you make the effort to define a parameter, you can try using it. As you can see, parameters are stored within a list called `params`. Each parameter is a named object of the list, so you can call it using the familiar operator `$`.

To see your report appear, you can both run it with the custom control on the RStudio interface or run the `render` function from the `rmarkdown` package, specifying in this case that the parameter's value needs to be selected by the user. As you can guess, you could also pass their value within the `render` function with a script similar to the following one:

```
render("parametrixed_report.Rmd", params = list(stock= c("GOOGL"))
```

This can actually be a useful trick if you need to automate the production of reports. For instance, at a specific closing date, you may have to produce some reports on different subsidiaries of your company. You could write a loop to run this function once for each of your subsidiaries:

```
library(rmakdown)
subsidiaries <- c("alpha","beta","gamma)
for (i in 1:subsidiaries){
render("parametrized_report.Rmd", params = list(company=
subsidiaries[i])
}
```

The preceding code will produce a report in your working directory for each subsidiary. Isn't that great? Who is still saying R is just for statistical analysis?

There's more...

Parametrized reports are on the very edge of R Markdown development. You will therefore not find a lot of material on them. Nevertheless, I suggest that you check out the official R Markdown website at `http://rmarkdown.rstudio.com/` for updated articles and documentation.

Developing a single-file Shiny app

Shiny apps probably were one of the most game-changing products developed by RStudio.

These apps, because of their ability to link the analytical environment to the production one, are great instruments in the hands of developers and researchers interested in transforming their work into an actual data-driven product.

In this recipe, I will introduce you to the single-file app, which is becoming the standard for Shiny app development.

When Shiny was first introduced, apps had to be composed of two separate files: one for the user interface and another for the server logic.

Among several refinements and improvements, the RStudio team later introduced a way to produce a Shiny app contained within a single R script. This app is named *app.R*.

Getting ready

First, we need to install the Shiny package and load it in the R environment:

```
Install.packages('shiny')
library(shiny)
```

How to do it...

1. Create an `app.R` file.
2. Add a call to the Shiny package:
   ```
   library(shiny)
   ```
3. Create a `ui` object:
   ```
   ui <- fluidPage()
   ```

4. Create a `server` object:

```
server ← function(input,output) { }
```

5. Define a `reactive` data frame:

```
dataset <- reactive({
    subset(iris,iris$Species == input$species  & iris$Petal.Length
>= input$range[1] & iris$Petal.Length <= input$range[2])
  })
```

6. Define a table object within your server, depending on the data frame:

```
output$table <- renderTable({dataset()})
```

7. Define a plot object within your server, depending on the data frame:

```
output$plot <- renderPlot({
    plot(x=dataset()$Sepal.Length,y=dataset()$Sepal.Width)
```

8. Add a title to your `ui` object:

```
h1("custom filtering and visualization of your dataset"),
```

9. Add a brief description of your app:

```
p("using this app you can easily filter the iris dataset, choosing
which species
    to show and which range of Sepal.Length to consider"),
```

10. Add a radio button control to your UI to select a species:

```
radioButtons('species',label='select the species you want to focus
on',c("virginica","versicolor","setosa"),),
```

11. Add a slider control to filter the data frame based on the `Petal.Length` value:

```
sliderInput('range', label= 'select a range for Petal.Length
attribute',min= 1,max = 6.9, value = c(1,6.9)),
```

12. Add a plot output to your `ui` object:

```
plotOutput('plot'),
```

13. Add a table output to your `ui` object:

```
tableOutput('table')
```

14. Execute your code:

```
Source("app.R")
```

15. Run your app:

```
shinyApp(ui=ui,server=server)
```

Running this code will make your Shiny application show up:

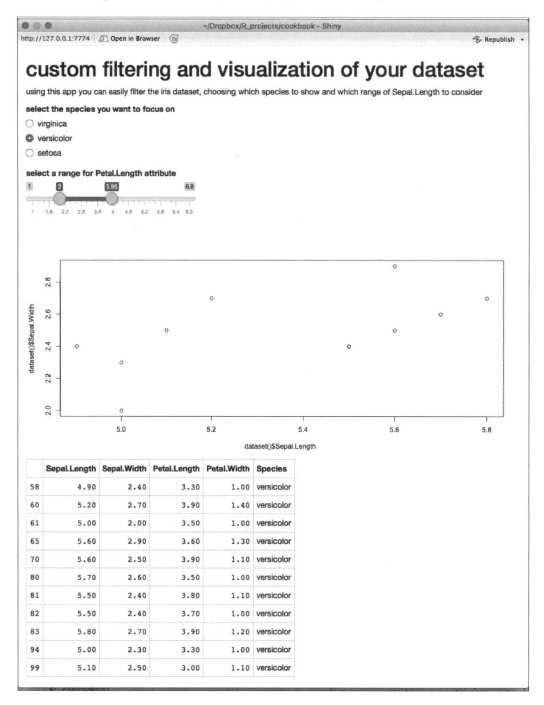

How it works...

We first created an R file that will contain all the code to compose your Shiny app. Be aware that naming the file `app.R` is mandatory.

The call to the Shiny package will make Shiny functions available to the app environment.

The logical framework behind Shiny requires every app to be composed of two main parts:

- **User interface (UI)**: This shows the user all available input controls and all elaboration results
- **Server logic**: This actually contains the code that reacts to user inputs and prepares the results to be shown to the user

We thus initialized the user interface of our app.

We then initialized the server logic of our app, which is defined as a function that has an argument input and output.

- `input`: This stores all user choices, captured from the input controls on the user interface
- `output`: This stores all the object resulting from server elaboration, making them available to the user interface

The two arguments are assumed to be of the `list` type.

The next step involves a core concept of the Shiny framework: **reactivity**. Reactivity is the ability to intercept user choices and actions, and consequently trigger pieces of code and concatenate pieces of code if any.

Let's visualize the flow:

- In the UI, the user specifies a choice, for instance, `within the iris dataset, let me see only the observation pertaining to the versicolor species.`
- Within the server logic, a `reactive()` function intercepts this choice and reacts to it, filtering the `iris` dataset accordingly and giving us an output of a dataset object of the data frame type.
- Still within the server logic, a `renderplot()` function reacts to the `reactive()` function filtering, since it has the dataset object within its brackets. The `renderplot()` function takes this modified dataset object as an input and gives a plot object as an output.
- On the UI side, a `plotOutput` function reacts to the change of plot object on the server side, since it has this object as an argument. Consequently, `plotOutput` shows a plot for the iris dataset filtered on the versicolor species.

That's it. The user's choice generates a long chain of actions and reactions that produce the final updated output.

However, here are two warnings:

- The `reactive()` function must include curly brackets, for instance, `reactive({ iris})`
- When you refer to the output of a reactive function, you need to add a `()` token on the right-hand side of the object, for instance, `Dataset()`

If you want to select an attribute of the object, you could add the usual dollar symbol or squared brackets.

We then created a table object that will let us show our filtered dataset to the user. Be aware of the use of `renderTable({})`, which is a special case of the more general `reactive()` function. We then defined a plot object, leveraging the `renderPlot({})` function.

We then skipped to the `ui` side, adding a title.

You can write text using the following functions:

- `H1()`
- `H2()`
- `H3()`
- `H4()`
- `H5()`
- `H6()`
- `P()`

While the first six functions are equivalent to the HTML title's tags, the last one is a general function for paragraph writing, corresponding to the HTML `<p>...</p>` tag.

We then used the `p()` function shown earlier.

Next, we actually added an input control, in the form of a radio button, which required us to perform only one choice among many.

We specified the following:

- The ID of the control to be used within the server logic to retrieve choices performed by the user
- The label, a piece of text to be shown to the user to help them make a choice
- The available choices, in the form of a vector
- The default choice

In a way similar to what we have done with the radio buttons, we add a slider control to let the user specify a range for the `Petal.Length` variable of the iris dataset. The main difference here is the presence of a minimum and maximum value, used to specify the available range of choice.

In the UI, we add two functions that will let us show the plot defined in the server logic named `plot` and the table named `table`.

In order to see your app, you have to execute your code to actually make the `ui` and `server` objects available within the environment.

Running your app just requires you to run a line of code in which you specify which objects Shiny should consider as `ui` and `server` objects.

See also

▶ Shiny apps deserved a separate section of the RStudio website at `http://shiny.rstudio.com`.

  In this website, you can find a lot of learning material to get you up and running with Shiny, from easy tutorials to advanced topics.

▶ In particular, I suggest that you further explore the UI controls that are available, in the reference section and the UI controls subsection: `http://shiny.rstudio.com/reference/shiny/latest/`.

Changing a Shiny app UI based on user input

Employing tools acquired in the previous recipe, you will be able to go quite far exploring Shiny's possibilities.

However, there is a quite advanced topic that was excluded from the previous recipe: UI customization based on user input.

This is an amazing feature, and it is even more amazing if you think you don't have to learn JavaScript or any other language to apply it to your app. Only R code knowledge is needed. Our app will ask for a first question and consequently change the possible answers to a second question.

One last word; our app will be based on the Lord of the Rings characters. I hope you will appreciate this. Now, let's start without any ado; as Samwise Gamgee would say:

> *"It's the job that's never started as takes longest to finish."*

Getting ready

In order to run our Shiny app, we will need to install and load the `shiny` and `shinyBS` packages:

```
Install.packages(c('shiny','shinyBS'))
library(shinyBS)
library(shiny)
```

Before looking at the actual recipe, I would like to recommend that you read the *Developing a single-file Shiny app* recipe in this chapter, which will help you gain knowledge of the basic features of the Shiny framework.

How to do it...

1. Create an `app.R` file. You just have to create a new R script within your current directory and name it `app.R`.

2. Create a `ui` object:

    ```
    ui <- fluidPage()
    ```

3. Create a `server` object:

    ```
    server <- function(input,output) { }
    ```

4. Put input controls into the UI:

    ```
    selectInput("first_choice",
                label = h1("First Answer a General Question"),
                choices = list("select","A","B","C"),
                selected = "select"
    ),

    #collapsable panel for second choice

    h1("then get into details"),

    bsCollapse(
      bsCollapsePanel( title = "details",
                       uiOutput("second_choice")
      ),
      id = "collapser", multiple = FALSE, open = NULL
    ),
    h2("first answer"),
    h3(textOutput("first_answer")),
    h2("second answer"),
    h3(textOutput("second_answer"))
    ```

Within this chunk of code, you should notice collapsible panels have been inserted using the `bsCollapse()` function made available through the `shinyBs` package we previously installed.

5. Put the server logic behind the UI's `input` control:

```
#retrieve selected values and render text from selection

output$first_answer  <- renderText({input$first_choice})
output$second_answer <- renderText({input$dynamic})
output$second_choice <- renderUI({

    switch(input$first_choice,
            "A" = checkboxGroupInput("dynamic", "Dynamic",
                                      choices = c("Aragon","Frodo"),
                                      selected = "option2"),
            "B" = checkboxGroupInput("dynamic", "Dynamic",
                                      choices =
c("Bilbo","Gandalf","Sauron"),
                                      selected = "option2"),
            "C" = checkboxGroupInput("dynamic", "Dynamic",
                                      choices =
c("Boromir","Legolas"),
                                      selected = "option2")

    )

})
```

In this chunk of code, we add server logic to the previously defined UI. You should notice the `renderUI()` reactive function, which is the actual core of this recipe.

This function takes `input$first_choice` as input, which is the first choice performed by the user using control having the `first_choice` ID (look at the previous step). This choice is used to select one of three cases listed within the `switch()` function. The output of this function is one of three possible `checkboxGroupInput`, which are then retrieved in the `uiOUtput()` UI function (refer to the previous step again).

6. Add an observer related to the first input:

```
observe({
    if (input$first_choice != "select") {
      updateCollapse(session,"collapser",open = c('details'))
    }
})
```

Observers are special types of reactive function. These functions can be considered always-active sentinels, which look for specific events (here, the value of `input$first_choice`) and consequently perform some action (here, collapsible panel update).

The main difference between general reactive functions and observers is that observers do not produce an output value, but just perform an action.

7. Run the UI and server lines.

   This step involves running the lines of code related to the `ui` and `server` objects. It is mandatory in order to make these objects available for the upcoming `shinyApp()` function.

   You can do this by sourcing your code file:

   ```
   source('app.R')
   ```

8. Run your Shiny app:

   ```
   shinyApp(ui = ui, server = server)
   ```

   This will result in the following app:

As you can see, after playing for a while with the app, choices within the second input control (then get into details one) will change based on the input of the first choice.

This is exactly what we were looking for: a dynamic UI able to change according to custom behavior.

See also

Shiny apps are a hot topic within the R community, particularly for the opportunity they offer for moving R closer to the data analytics production environment. You can, therefore, find a lot of great material on this topic online.

That said, if you want to deepen you knowledge of Shiny apps, you shouldn't miss visiting the following:

- ▶ The official Shiny app website at `http://shiny.rstudio.com`.

  In this website, you can find everything, from introductory tutorials for beginners to detailed articles on advanced topics.

- ▶ A specific guide on the topic of dynamic UI is retrievable from `http://shiny.rstudio.com/articles/dynamic-ui.html`.

- ▶ If you then would like to experience Shiny's potential, you can look at the Shiny gallery at `http://shiny.rstudio.com/gallery/`.

Creating an interactive report with Shiny

This recipe gives you a perfect tool for sharing analysis results with third parties.

Interactive reports are electronic documents enriched by Shiny functionalities, giving the user the ability to change the assumptions on which analyses are based and consequently changing the document's output.

You should now be comfortable with your analysis, autonomously answering questions that arise while reading.

How to do it...

1. Create a Shiny document:

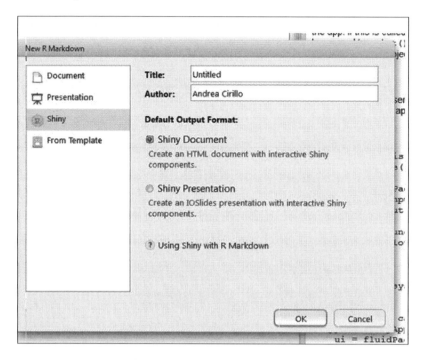

2. Remove the default content `yaml` parameters.

3. Add a `setup` chunk:

````
```{r setup, include=FALSE}
knitr::opts_chunk$set(echo = TRUE)
```
````

4. Embed your Shiny app:

````
```{r tabsets, echo=FALSE}
shinyAppDir(
  "app.R",
  options = list(
    width = "100%", height = 550
  )
)
```
````

5. Add an input panel and a related plot output:

```r
```{r eruptions, echo=FALSE}
inputPanel(
  selectInput("selected_species", label = "iris species to plot",
              choices = c("virginica","setosa","versicolor"),
  selected = "versicolor")

)
data <- reactive({
  subset(iris,iris$Species == input$selected_species)
})
renderPlot({
  plot(data())
})
```
```

6. Style your document.

How it works...

We first create a Shiny document. Shiny documents are actually R Markdown documents where an additional `render` argument is set to `shiny`. This argument is specified within the `yaml` chunk, as seen in the *Using one markup language for all types of documents – rmarkdown* recipe.

Next, we remove the default content, except the `yaml` parameters.

We don't want the default content to confuse us, do we? So, let's clean up our paper, leaving only our dear `yaml` chunk.

Next, we add a setup chunk. Setup chunks are chunks of R code where some general and preliminary activities are performed, such as package loading and data frame importing. Take a look at the *Using one markup language for all types of documents – rmarkdown* recipe.

We then embed our Shiny app. There are two ways of embedding a Shiny app in your document:

► Embedding a previously developed Shiny app in your document by leveraging `shinyAppDir()`

► Introducing `inputpanel` and a consequent `ui` element, such as plots or tables

The second option is treated in the next step, while here we source our previously developed app, passing only the relative path, since it is placed in the project directory.

Be aware of the option can specify within the `options` argument, which is the same as that available for the `runApp` function (see `runApp` for more on them), plus specific controls for the width and height of the app shown in your document.

Further on, add an input panel and a related plot output.

This is a fairly specific way of using the Shiny framework, since we don't have to specify any `server` object or `ui` object to use control widgets and output objects.

The logical model behind this implementation is in some way different from the general approach in the following ways:

> ▶ An input panel is required to store all control widgets, meaning all those elements that will appear in the document to let the user perform choices such as data filtering or model assumptions

> ▶ Using a render function to show the results of user choices, such as `renderPlot` and `renderTable`

What is missing here? The output function. For instance, when dealing with a plot, you will not require a `plotOutput` function, since the `renderplot` function will do the job.

Lastly, we style our document. As we discussed at the beginning of this recipe, Shiny documents are R Markdown documents empowered by Shiny framework functionalities. This means you can leverage all the great features of R Markdown documents to style and customize your report. Refer to the *Using one markup language for all types of documents – rmarkdown* recipe for further information on this topic.

See also

As usual with Shiny, the sky is the limit. Given the relatively young age of the framework, a lot of development is still to come.

I suggest that you always keep an eye on the Shiny website, especially for this particular topic, on the section in the R Markdown website dedicated to Shiny at `http://rmarkdown.rstudio.com/authoring_shiny.html`.

Constructing RStudio add-ins

RStudio add-ins are one of the newest and most promising developments introduced recently by the RStudio team. They add infinite possibilities for improvement to users' workflows through the enhancement of their IDE.

There are two main types of add-ins:

> ▶ **Text macros**: These only produce a text insertion within your code (for instance the `()` `{}` structure to be added after the `function` token).

> ▶ **Shiny gadgets**: These are little Shiny apps that are shown within the viewer pane, a pop-up window, or a browser window. They let you perform advanced activities such as statistical parameter definition or data-wrangling tasks.

In this example, we will develop the second type of add-in from the function definition, for deployment and installation as a package on GitHub.

Our example will be a funny one: we will develop an add-in that lets you see weather forecasts for a specified city within the R console.

Getting ready

Let's first install the `shiny` and `miniUI` packages:

```
install.packages(c("shiny", "miniUI"), type = "source")
library(shiny)
library(miniUI)
```

How to do it...

1. Define the function that will be called from your add-in:

   ```
   weatheraddin <-function (){}
   ```

2. Define your `ui` add-in:

   ```
   ui <- miniPage(
     gadgetTitleBar("weather forecasts"),
     miniContentPanel(
       textInput("city","input your city name", value = "milan")
     )
   )
   ```

3. Define your `server` add-in:

   ```
   server <- function(input,output,session){
     observeEvent(input$done, {
       weather_command <- paste0("finger ",input$city,"@graph.no")
       system(weather_command)
       stopApp()
     })
   }
   ```

4. Define where your add-in will be displayed:

   ```
   runGadget(ui, server, viewer = dialogViewer("weather forecasts add in"))
   ```

5. Try your add-in:

   ```
   weatheraddin()
   ```

6. Put your add-in in a package.

   RStudio offers a custom type of `rproj` for packages. Therefore, in order to create a new R package, you will just need to create a new project and select the **R Package** option:

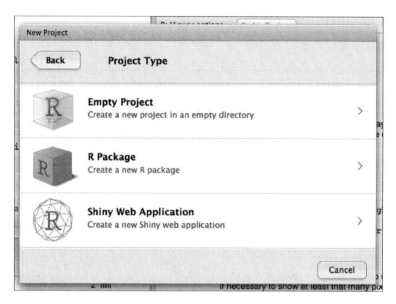

After choosing this option, the following window will show up, asking you whether any source code is available on which to base the package:

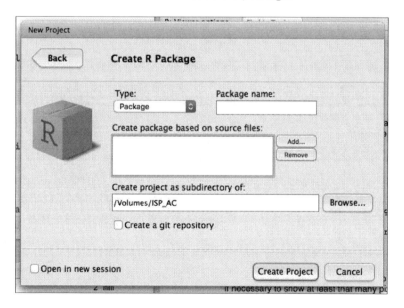

By clicking on the **Add...** button, you will be able to select the R file containing the add-in function. For the purpose of the recipe, we provided a separate R file containing our weather add-in function named `addin_source.R`.

The R package which will result from this procedure is a package ready for distribution.

7. Host your package on GitHub.

   We'll create a repository on the GitHub website to make it available for distribution and remote downloading by a potential user.

   You can learn how to host an RStudio project within a GitHub repository by reading the *Using GitHub with RStudio* recipe in *Chapter 5, Power Programming with R*.

8. Install your package and try your add-in. In order to install your package, we will leverage the `install_github()` function from the `devtools` package, which you should have already installed from the getting ready section (if not, you can always skip back to that section; I will wait for you here).

   Once you are done, you can just run the following command:

   ```
   install_github("andreacirilloac/weather_addin_package")
   load(weather_addin_package)
   ```

   Substitute `andreacirilloac` with your GitHub username.

9. Create an `addins.dcf` file.

   To register your add-in in the RStudio IDE, you will have an `addins.dcf` file located within your project directory, in a path similar to the following one: `project_directory/inst/rstudio/addins.dcf`.

   The `addins.dcf` file is the file where installed add-ins are recorded and used by RStudio in order to define which functions have to be treated as add-ins rather than as simple functions. Feed your `addins.dcf` file.

   Installing your add-in will result in the add-in menu showing your add-in, as in the following screenshot:

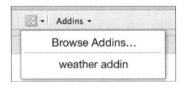

In order to obtain this, you will have to locate the `addins.dcf` file and insert the following lines into this file:

```
Name: weather addin
Description: show weather forecasts within R console
Binding: weatheraddin
Interactive: false
/inst/rstudio/addins.dcf
```

This piece of text will be separated from the previous one by a blank line.

There's more...

Having an RStudio add-in that lets you find out weather forecasts can be funny, but I don't really think you are going to consider it useful, unless you are a meteorologist, of course. In all the remaining cases, you should consider this recipe as an explanatory example, using it as a base to develop your custom add-in.

Sharing your work on RPubs

RPubs is the logical end of the path that starts with an R script:

- ▸ Development of R code
- ▸ Development of an R Markdown report embedding the R code
- ▸ Publishing and sharing your R Markdown report online

One of the greatest advantages of RPubs is its good integration with the RStudio environment.

We will see how to publish your analyses on RPubs from the ground up.

Getting ready

In order to publish your work on RPubs, you will first have to create an account on this portal.

To sign up on RPubs, you just have to navigate to `http://rpubs.com/users/new`.

The signing-up procedure will ask you to fill in some fields.

After filling in the required fields, you will get an account on the platform, and you will be ready to publish your first report on RPubs.

In this recipe, we will publish one of the reports produced in our previous recipes, and specifically the parametrized reports produced in the *Generating dynamic parametrized reports with R Markdown* recipe in this chapter.

How to do it...

1. Hit the publish button in RStudio in the upper-right corner of the source editor:

2. Insert the document details:

3. Enjoy your document online:

4. Share your document:

There's more...

You should have noticed that every published document comes with a **Comments** button, which lets you see whether someone has commented on your work. This feature, based on the Disqus platform, is particularly useful when your publication is aimed at stimulating exchanges of opinion around a topic linked to your work.

Deploying your app on Amazon AWS with ramazon

RStudio offers a great facility for Shiny apps deployment, named `shinyapps.io`. This hosting web platform is perfectly integrated with RStudio and lets you deploy your app by hitting a button. You can find convenient tutorials at `http://shiny.rstudio.com/articles/shinyapps.html`.

A large number of developers are used to the structure and facilities of Amazon AWS, which provides an integrated and solid framework for web application deployment.

Amazon AWS is one of the best-known services of its kind. However, publishing apps on it can be laborious for non-expert users, requiring you to remotely log in on a Linux server and perform terminal downloading and installation activities. That is why I have developed the `ramazon` package, which lets you publish a Shiny application on Amazon simply by running a function. This recipe exposes the usage of the package.

Getting ready

In order to install a Shiny server on Amazon AWS, you first need to create an EC2 instance on Amazon AWS. This basically means you will have to create an up and running Linux server on which you can host your Shiny application. If you need help with this, I have provided a detailed tutorial on how to do this at `http://www.slideshare.net/AndreaCirillo1/how-to-launch-an-aws-ec2-instance-51349866?ref=https://andreacirilloblog.wordpress.com/2015/08/18/deploy-your-shiny-app-on-aws-with-a-function/`.

How to do it...

1. Retrieve your server public DNS from Amazon AWS:

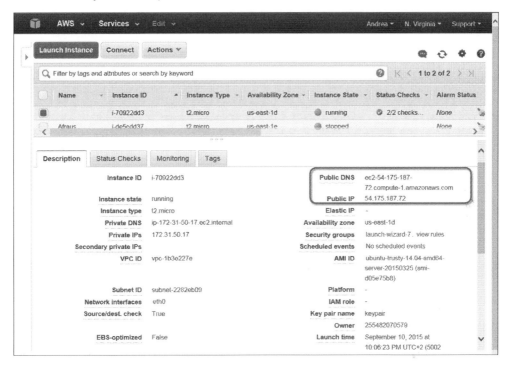

2. Retrieve your server key from Amazon AWS:

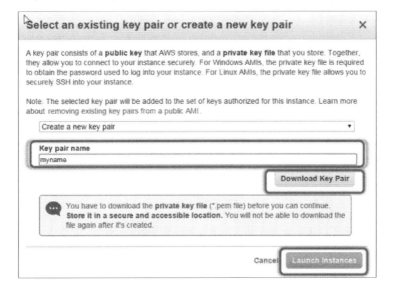

3. Install the `ramazon` package from GitHub.

   Currently, the `ramazon` package is only available through GitHub. In order to use it, you will have to execute the following code. This code installs `devtools`, which lets you download `ramazon` from the GitHub repo:

   ```
   install.packages("devtools")
   library(devtools)
   install_github("andreacirilloac/ramazon")
   library(ramazon)
   ```

4. Run `ramazon()`.

   ```
   ramazon(public_DNS ="your_Public_DNS", key_pair_name = "your_key_
   pair_name")
   ```

5. Enjoy your app.

Index

A

alternative function's performance
  comparing, microbenchmarking package
      used 129-131
Amazon AWS
  app developing on, ramazon used 222-224
API
  accessing, with R 12-16
  endpoints 15
app
  deploying on Amazon AWS, ramazon
      used 222-224
**Autoregressive integrated moving average
  (Arima) 173**
axes
  customizing, to ggplot2 plot 74-79

B

Benford's law
  used for detecting fraud on e-commerce
      orders 156-161
blog
  curating, through RStudio 190-195

C

callback URL 15
character_wise search
  performing, with twitteR 18
chunk options
  reference link 182
code
  sharing, with slides 188-190

code performance
  evaluating, with profvis package 126-128
Code School 139
cohort analysis
  used, for measuring customers retention
      in R 161-163
Colors in R
  URL 74
communities
  displaying, in network with linkcomm
      package 93-97
CSS selector 3
customers retention
  measuring, with cohort analysis in R 161-163
custom objects and methods, R
  creating, S3 system used 123-125

D

data
  acquiring, from Web 2-11
  cleansing 34
  displaying, with plot() function 60-66
  filtering activities, performing 48-58
  format 2
  getting from Facebook, Rfacebook package
      used 21-23
  getting, from Google Analytics 24-27
  getting from Twitter, twitteR package
      used 16-21
  license 2
  loading into R, with rio packages 27-31
  manipulating 34
  preparing for anyalysis, tidyr package
      used 36-40

structure 34-36
degree 92
DiagrammeR package
used, for producing process flow diagram in
RStudio 112-115
dynamic force network
creating, with visNetwork package 104-110
dynamic parametrized reports
creating, R Markdown used 198-204
dynamic UI
URL 213

F

Fiat-Chrysler Automotive stock price 173
file formats
converting, rio package used 31, 32
forecast()
reference link 167
used, for exploring time series
forecasting 167, 168
fraud, on e-commerce orders
detecting, with Benford' s law 156-160

G

geom_text() function 74
ggmap
URL 88
used, for drawing route on map 85-88
ggplot2 plot
axes, customizing 74-79
matrix of graphs, producing 79-85
text, adding at custom location 69-74
Git
download link 131
interactive tutorial, reference link 139
GitHub
about 131
reference link 191
URL 13
using, with RStudio 131-139
Google Analytics
data, getting from 24-27
URL 24, 27

Google Query explorer
URL 26
Grammar of Graphics
reference link 72

H

HTML tags
URL 11
HyperText Markup Language (HTML 8

I

If This ThenThat (IFTTT) 12
igraph package
about 88
used, for drawing network 88-93
ImageMagick
about 110
reference link 110
interactive report
creating, Shiny app used 213-216
interactive visualizations
using 100
Internet of Things (IoT) 2

L

linkcomm package
about 93
used, for displaying communities in
network 93-97

M

Mactex
reference link 184
map
route, drawing with ggmap 85-88
Markdown
reference link 184
syntax 177
matrix of graphs
producing, with ggplot2 plot 79-85
Medici
reference link 92

mice package
  URL 47
  used, for substituting missing values 43-47
microbenchmarking package
  used, for comparing alternative function's
      performance 129, 130
Miktext
  reference link 184
missing values
  detecting 40-43
  removing 40-43
  substituting, mice package used 43-47
modular code
  writing, in RStudio 118-120
multiple imputation technique 43

N

NaN (not a number) 40
network
  communities, displaying with linkcomm
      package 93-97
  drawing, igraph package used 88-93
networkD3 package
  used, for producing Sankey diagram 100-104
nottem 165

O

OAuth
  URL 13
outliers
  detecting 47, 48
  removing 47, 48

P

pairs.panels()function
  used, for visualizing correlations between
      variables 67-69
parallel computation
  implementing, in R 120-123
PDF documents
  styling, with RStudio 184, 185
  writing, with RStudio 184, 185

PDF reports, folder
  analyzing, with tm package 143-147
pdftotext
  download link 144
plot() function
  used, for displaying data 60-66
plots
  sharing, with slides 188-190
Portfolio Analytics package
  used, for maximising return 170-172
  used, for optimizing portfolio
      composition 170, 171
profvis package
  used, for evaluating code
      performance 126-128

Q

quantmod package
  reference link 168
  used, for tracking stock movements 168, 169

R

R
  custom objects and methods, creating with
      S3 system 123-125
  parallel computation, implementing 120-123
  used, for accessing API 12-16
ramazon
  used, for developing app on Amazon
      AWS 222-224
RColorBrewer package
  URL 74
recommendation engine
  creating 163, 164
regular expressions
  dealing with 142
repository 131
results sharing phase 175
Revolution Analytics
  reference link 120
Rfacebook package
  used, for getting data from Facebook 21-23

rio package
used, for converting file formats 31, 32
used, for loading data into R 27-31
Rio vignette
URL 30
R Markdown
about 177-179
reference link 184
URL 204
used, for creating dynamic parametrized
    reports 198-204
used, for writing tufte handouts 186-188
working 180-183
rmarkdown-website
reference link 194
rotating 3D graph
building 110-112
exporting, as GIF 110-112
route() function, arguments
alternatives 87
from 87
messaging 87
mode 87
output 87
override_limit 87
sensor 87
structure 87
to 87
RPubs
URL 220
work, sharing 220-222
RStudio
blog, curating through 190-195
DiagrammeR package, used for process
    flow diagram production 112-115
GitHub, using with 131-139
modular code, writing 118-120
URL 11, 209, 222
used, for styling PDF documents 184, 185
used, for writing PDF documents 184, 185
RStudio add-ins
connecting 216-220
Shiny gadgets 216
text macros 216
rvest
URL 13

S

S3 system
used, for creating custom objects and
    models in R 123-125
Sankey diagram
producing, with networkD3 package 100-104
SelectorGadget
about 3
URL 4
setup chunk 181
Shell 133
Shiny app
framework, reactivity 207
framework 112
gallery, URL 213
server logic 207
single file Shiny app, developing 204-209
tutorial, URL 222
UI changing, based on user inputs 209-213
URL 213
used, for creating interactive report 213-216
user interface (UI) 207
single-file Shiny app
developing 204-209
slides
used, for sharing codes 188-190
used, for sharing plots 188-190
stl() function
used, for performing time series
    decomposition 165, 166
stock market
forecasting 173, 174
stock movements
tracking, quantmod package used 168, 169
stock parameter 203

T

task view
reference link 123
Texlive
reference link 184
text
adding, to ggplot2 plot at custom
    location 69-74

Tidy data
URL 40
tidyr package
used, for preparing data with analysis 36-40
time series decomposition
performing, stl() function used 165, 166
remainder 165
seasonal component 165
trend component 165
time series forecasting
exploring, with forecast() 167, 168
tm package
used for analyzing PDF reports in
folder 143-147
tufte handouts
writing, with rmarkdown 186, 187
writing, with tufte handouts 186-188
tufte package
used, for writing tufte handouts 186-188
twitteR package
used, for getting data from Twitter 16-20
Twitter sentiment analysis
performing 151-155

U

UI controls
URL 209
Unix timestamp 23

V

variables
correlations, visualizing with pairs.panels()
function 67-69
visNetwork package
reference link 110
used, for creating dynamic force
network 104-110

W

web scraping tasks 2-11
website
reference link 195
wget installation, for Unix OS
reference link 191
wide format 37
Windows OS
reference link 191
wordclouds
creating, with wordcloud package 148-150
work
sharing, on RPubs 220-222

Y

Your Access Token 17

Printed in Great Britain
by Amazon